BOWLER HATS AND STETSONS

Joshua Norton – 'Emperor of the United States and Protector of Mexico' (*Author's collection.*)

Bowler Hats
and
Stetsons

Stories of Englishmen
in the Wild West

Colin Rickards

RONALD WHITING AND WHEATON
London

FOR

MOTHER and FATHER

WITH LOVE

First published
in Great Britain 1966
by
Ronald Whiting & Wheaton Ltd
106 Gt Portland Street
London W1

Printed and bound
in Great Britain by
A Wheaton & Co Ltd
Exeter Devon

CONTENTS

BOOK ONE

BOOK TWO

ILLUSTRATIONS

PREFACE

The British contribution to the opening up of the American West was a large one.

British capital – particularly during the 1880s and 1890s – financed some of the biggest ranches in Texas, Colorado and Montana and many settlers flocked to take advantage of the free land.

Even before that men of British birth fought with gallantry and distinction in the Mexican War of 1846 and on both sides in the bloody Civil War between the divided nation in 1861–65. Nearly a fifth of the garrison who fell at the Alamo, to win in blood the independence of Texas in 1836, were British.

In this book I have told just a few of the stories of Englishmen – and women – in the American West. They are colourful tales of migrants in a new and untamed country, what the late President Kennedy has called 'A Nation of Immigrants'.

ACKNOWLEDGEMENTS

Many people have generously given their time to help me collect material from various sources and to them all I wish to express my thanks. Dr C. L. Sonnichsen, of the Texas Western College, El Paso, Texas, offered encouragement from the very beginning and put me on to one story I might otherwise have missed; Barry C. Johnson, of London, let me loose in his extensive library and offered advice on many matters; G. Derek West, of Tunbridge Wells, provided information from his personal files which saved me a great deal of time; Chris Penn, of London, pointed out several leads which I had overlooked; Waldo Koop, of Wichita, Kansas, supplied information on a number of points; Nyle H. Miller, Secretary of the Kansas State Historical Society, Topeka, Kansas, most generously shared information he had collected over a number of years; Miss Alberta Pantle, Librarian of the same Society, provided additional information; Bernard R. Carman, of Schenectady, New York, gave some pointers; Mrs Laura Allyn Ekstrom, Librarian of the State Historical Society of Colorado, dug out material from their files for me; Raymond W. Thorp, of Norwalk, California, took time off from his own researches to tell me the story of his father, James Thorp; Arthur Kent, of London, pointed out an excellent story I would otherwise have missed; Joseph G. Rosa, of Ruislip, Middlesex, author and friend, lent me source material from his personal collection; Jeffrey Burton, of London, gave me advice on several occasions; Mrs Irene Simpson, Director of the Wells Fargo Bank History Room, San Francisco, California, provided material from their files; Mrs Eve Ball, of Hollywood, New Mexico, gave me access to her own researches and fund of knowledge of early New Mexico; to Mrs Meena Stentiford and Miss Lillian Locke, who managed to turn a very untidy original draft into carefully-typed manuscript, I owe perhaps the greatest debt of all.

To the old friends who helped and the new ones I made in writing this book, my sincere thanks. Any merits it has are due to them. The rest I take upon myself.

COLIN RICKARDS.

London, October, 1965.

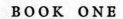
BOOK ONE

BOOK ONE

CHAPTER ONE

THE ENGLISHMAN IN THE WEST

THE Englishman who came to the West was a peer or a commoner; a wealthy investor or a poverty-stricken emigrant; a law abiding citizen or a crook. He was typical of the early day settler. He made a place for himself, and often his family, on a wild and dangerous frontier. And, having found his chosen niche, he stayed there, come hell or high water.

Much of the crime wave in San Francisco of the Gold Rush days could be laid at the door of the English. But not the English emigrant. For the infamous gang of robbers and cut-throats known as 'The Sydney Ducks', though English, had come from the penal settlements of Australia either as freed criminals or escaped ones.

In 1848, when James Marshall discovered gold in the mill creek of his Swiss employer John Sutter, he set in motion the California Gold Rush. The following year some 75,000 men arrived in California from every state and territory in the United States, from England, from Australia, from all over Europe and from as far afield as China, India and Japan. There was not another gold rush like it until the Klondyke strikes half a century later.

From the very beginning gangs of outlaws preyed on the honest miners and businessmen. It was easier to get rich by means of a gun, a knife or a club than to pan gold in the icy streams of the gold fields. The first large and well-organised gang were 'The Hounds', a motley collection of small-time criminals from New York's tough East Side. Mexican, Negro and Chinese miners were their special prey but it was a four-hundred strong band of white miners who one summer's night in 1849 marched with torches on 'The Hounds' tent town and drove them from San Francisco.

The city's first jail was a derelict barque, the *Euphemia*, which lay in the mud in the harbour. The first sheriff was John C. Hays, a tough former Texas Ranger.

'The Hounds' had departed for fresh fields. But in their place came 'The Sydney Ducks', desperadoes from the Australian prison settlements. And their bold robberies and vicious attacks had all San Francisco on edge.

By the middle of 1850 the respectable citizenry had had enough. Led by newspaperman Sam Brannan they formed a Vigilante Committee on lines which were to become almost standard throughout the West for the rest of the century. A firebell was sounded whenever the 250-strong band of Vigilantes was needed.

Soon afterwards one of 'The Sydney Ducks' was captured while stealing a safe.

'Every lover of liberty lay hold of a rope,' yelled Sam Brannan and the highwayman was hoisted into Eternity.

In May, 1850, the firebell clanged again and the Vigilantes assembled to deal with James Stuart, a young Englishman, despite his Scottish name, who had been arrested after the particularly brutal beating and robbery of citizen C. J. Jansen. Stuart, known as 'English Jim', was already wanted by the police for escaping from the Sacramento jail in which he had been held for the murder of Sheriff Moore of the town of Auburn. 'English Jim' had been picked off the streets the day after the Jansen robbery and the injured citizen identified him at once.

But the man they thought was 'English Jim' Stuart identified himself as Thomas Berdue, late of London and later still of Australia. He poured out a tale of his recent arrival from Australia where he had left a devoted wife and family while he came to seek his fortune.

Berdue was tried by the Vigilante court. The prosecutor itemized his crimes and when the man swore that he was not 'English Jim' the prosecutor gave the jury a detailed description of the badman. It tallied with Berdue to an uncanny degree. Both men were the same height; both had brown hair and were thinning at the crown; the lobe of 'English Jim's' left ear was split, and so was Berdue's; the badman had a deformed finger and so did Berdue; both men wore the same style of beard. But what clinched it was the fact that 'English Jim' had been a printer at one time and his fingers were permanently stained with printer's ink. Berdue, exhibiting his own ink-stained fingers, explained that he too had been in the printing trade.

When the verdict was handed to the judge after four hours the jury had split; nine voted 'guilty' and three voted 'not guilty'. The prisoner was sent to Marysville to stand trial again. This time, having partly beaten the case of the Jansen robbery, he was to face a jury for the murder of Sheriff Moore. He was found guilty and sentenced to hang.

Then, on 2nd July a man was arrested in San Francisco's dockland. Alert detectives immediately remembered Berdue's story. The prisoner and the man held as 'English Jim' were identical. Eventually the man broke down. He was, he confessed, 'English Jim' Stuart. Thomas Berdue was released from the Marysville jail and travelled to San Francisco.

And there, on 11th July, he watched the Vigilantes hang his 'double', 'English Jim' Stuart from the Market Street Wharf.

Other hangings followed as the Vigilantes, now thoroughly feared by the criminal element, proceeded to break up 'The Sydney Ducks'. By 1855 there was almost no more need for Vigilante justice. Law and order had been established and had come to stay.

The last action of the Vigilante Committee came in August, 1855, with the double hanging of New York badman Philander Brace and English-born murderer Joseph Hetherington.

Afterwards the Vigilantes, with Sam Brannan marching at the head of 5,000 citizens, paraded through the streets of San Francisco in a final and triumphant review before their disbandment.

Commented the correspondent of the London *Times*: 'Seldom do self-constituted authorities retire with grace and dignity, but it is due to the Vigilante Committee to say that they have done so.'

'The Sydney Ducks' were dead or scattered. But English outlawry in California had not come to a complete and abrupt end.

For an Englishman was to ride stirrup to stirrup with American-born outlaws and achieve the dubious notoriety of being with the first gang of bandits to try to rob a stagecoach in what

was to become the traditional manner of roadagents across the
West. It was a notable failure, but it set a pattern for others.

There arose in California in 1856 a highly successful small
gang led by one Dr Thomas J. Hodges, a brave and educated
man from Rome, Tennessee, with a fine war record as a self-
sacrificing doctor of the Tennessee Volunteers in the United
States war with Mexico. Just why he turned to crime is uncertain, but turn he did. In late 1855, under the name of Captain
Tom Bell, he was sentenced to a term of imprisonment for mule
theft. He escaped and teamed up with Will Gristy, an experienced criminal, to organise one of the first successful gangs
of roadagents in the Golden State.

One of the first men to flock to Bell's outlaw banner was a
young Englishman remembered in the ill-recorded history of the
period as English Bob Carr. Perhaps he was one of the displaced
'Sydney Ducks'. And again, perhaps he was not. Others in the
gang included Jim Smith, Ned Connor and Monte Jack Lyon.

The gang had been riding high, wide and handsome across the
California gold trails for several months relieving travellers of
their hard-dug gold when Captain Tom Bell heard that one of
the new Concord stages would be carrying $100,000 in gold dust
and nuggets on the run between Camptonville and Marysville.

The fact that nobody had ever held up a stagecoach was of
small importance to Bell and his gang, firm believers that there
has to be a first time for everything. They made their plans
and laid a trap near Marysville.

On 11th August, 1856, the stage left the Langton Express
Company's office at Camptonville on time. John Gear was in the
driver's seat and Bill Dobson sat beside him with a shotgun resting across his knees. The bullion box with $100,000 was chained
to the floor under their seat. Inside the coach rode nine passengers. Two were miners, two Marysville businessmen, Mrs
Tilghman the coloured wife of a Marysville barber, and four
Chinese labourers.

At Dry Creek Ford the bandits struck.

But Captain Bell's timing was wrong. As he, English Bob and
Monte Jack galloped from one side of the trail they realised
they were alone. Will Gristy and the other men should have
come at the stage from the other side. But they were not there.

Shotgun messenger Bill Dobson took one look at the three roughly dressed men with drawn guns and opened fire. His first shot knocked Bell from his horse. From where he lay Bell shot Dobson in the arm. Driver Gear whipped up his team and the stage raced on. A hundred yards down the road Will Gristy and his men appeared. They fired a volley of shots as the wildly swaying stage raced by. Inside the coach Mrs Tilghman slumped over dead and the two Marysville merchants cursed as they clutched gunshot wounds.

Tom Bell, only slightly wounded, led his men away from the scene of the abortive holdup.

Posses rode out of Marysville as soon as the news of the attempted robbery was known. The gang had split up but Will Gristy was captured and under threat of hanging gave the location of Tom Bell's hideout. Bell was not there when the posse reached a lonely cabin near Knight's Ferry. It took them some six weeks to catch up with him but Judge Belt who headed the law and order league in the district was a determined and patient man.

On 4th October, 1856, Captain Tom Bell sat on his horse under a tree with a bottle in his hand. There was a rope around his neck and when Bell had taken a long, last drink Judge Belt slapped the horse's rump and it jumped forward leaving the doctor from Tennessee treading air.

'English Bob' Carr was never caught. Perhaps he learned his lesson and turned to more honest pursuits.

Several years before Carr had embarked on his criminal career a fellow countryman had set out to become the richest of the Mississippi riverboat gamblers. It was an ambitious aim, but he succeeded.

The riverboats of the Mississippi were a gambler's paradise. The great river was the lifeline of the middle West and carried cargo and passengers in about equal amounts. Many of the passengers were wealthy businessmen, always ready for a game of cards – and always game for the professional card-sharps. The riverboat era was at its peak between 1845 and 1860 and some 1,500 gamblers operated on the five hundred steamers which operated up-river out of New Orleans. Their favourite prey were the rich planters, the slave owners and the foolish young scions of wealthy European families with bulging wallets and money-belts.

Young Dick Hargrove was not the scion of a wealthy family and his moneybelt was almost empty when he landed in New Orleans in 1844. The 16-year-old London boy had run away from home seeking adventure. He took a job cleaning out a bar in the tough dockland area and then went to work on the river-boats as a bartender. Less than a month later he won $25,000 in a poker game with a rich Louisiana cotton planter. It was the turning point in his life. He quit serving drinks and began order-ing them – from the gaming tables.

Unlike so many of his fellow gamblers, Dick Hargrove played square. He knew the odds favoured the professional and so he played a straight game. His reputation grew. So did his bankroll.

But Hargrove, in his black suit, extravagantly frilled white shirts, and colourful waistcoat, had just one weakness – women. He was a notorious lady-killer and his many amours often re-sulted in duels with lovers and husbands.

His most serious romantic escapade occurred in 1850 when he met and fell in love with the wife of a prominent New Orleans banker who found out what was going on and challenged him to a duel.

Hargrove killed the husband in a bowie knife duel. The woman's brother then swore to kill the gambler on sight. A year later they met in a gambling room at Natchez. The brother in-vited Hargrove to step outside. He obliged, and in the fight which followed beat the brother to death with his bare hands.

That night the woman slipped a knife from under the pillow and plunged it into the sleeping Hargrove's chest. She then turned it on herself. She died. The gambler recovered. He moved from New Orleans to Cuba and stayed there until the Civil War broke out. He served with distinction in the war between the States and ended up as a major in the Union Army.

Dick Hargrove went to live in Denver and enjoy his fortune. Just before he died of tuberculosis in 1880 he said that during his gambling life some $2 million had passed through his well-manicured hands.

But if the English were outlaws and gamblers at times, they were also lawmen.

William Smith, City Marshal of the rip-roaring cattle town of Wichita, Kansas, once gave the doughty Wyatt Earp a beating when that famous frontier marshal was a mere policeman.

Smith was born in Leicester on 22nd April, 1844, and lived in that city for the first nine years of his life. When his parents emigrated to America they first settled in Lawrence, Kansas, and then moved westward to take up free land near the small town of Manhattan.

Young William saw service against the Indians as a private in Company L, Eleventh Regiment, Kansas Volunteer Cavalry during the Civil War. He had joined up to fight the Confederates but his regiment was used instead to protect the frontier. He mustered out in 1865 and four years later began operating a sawmill in Wichita.

In 1870 he was defeated in the elections for Sedgwick County's first Sheriff but before the year was out he had been commissioned a Deputy United States Marshal. Smith sold his sawmill and opened the Star Livery Stable in Wichita. On 10th April, 1871, he was offered the post of City Marshal but declined it as he had already made arrangements to be out of town on business.

An Irishman, Mike Meagher, was appointed in his place and the following year William Smith obtained a commission as Deputy Sheriff of Sedgwick County under the Marshal's brother John. In 1873 John Meagher resigned his post and Kansas' Governor Thomas Osborn appointed Smith to fill the vacancy until the next elections in which he ran but was defeated.

Smith proved himself a skilled and able detective. On one occasion he tracked a murderer across three states, located him living under another name and returned him to Wichita to stand trial.

On 15th April, 1874, the City Council asked Smith to become City Marshal and this time he accepted.

The Wichita *Eagle* was delighted about the appointment and said: 'He made an excellent and popular Deputy Sheriff, and as City Marshal we have no doubt of his success.'

William Smith ran for re-election in 1875 but was defeated by ex-City Marshal Mike Meagher. The locals wanted a change. He continued to serve as a Deputy United States Marshal and had many arrests to his credit.

Wyatt Earp had by this time arrived in Wichita and was serving as a policeman. Contrary to his own boasts and claims he was never Marshal, merely a policeman, third or fourth in the city's four-man law enforcement set-up.

The campaign for the election of a City Marshal for 1876 was a lively one. William Smith and Mike Meagher were the contestants again and Wyatt Earp naturally had to support his superior. Unfortunately for him he became over enthusiastic and on 2nd April went to Smith's house to beat him up, presumably so that he would be out of action on polling day.

Earp was discharged from the police force for his attack on Smith who later lost the election. The City Council considered Earp for re-instatement but decided against it on a vote of six against him and only two for him. Several days later, because he now had no visible means of support, the vagrancy act was enforced against Wyatt Earp and his brother James. They bowed out of Wichita and headed for Dodge City.

William Smith left Wichita soon afterwards. He became the first mayor of Galena, Cherokee County, and was later postmaster. He died on 25th April, 1908.

Around the time William Smith was City Marshal of Wichita, another Englishman was seeing some pretty tough days in another part of Kansas.

In 1873 James W. Grahame was working as a scout for a surveying party attached to the Texas Pacific Railroad when he was a witness to one of the most talked of duels in the West.

The trouble had begun two years earlier when a Texan named Hugh Anderson shot and killed a night policeman in Newton, Kansas. The man's name was Mike McCluskey and the killing occurred in a Newton saloon. In the shoot-out nine men were killed or wounded and the frontiersmen spoke of the affair as 'The Newton General Massacre'. Mike McCluskey's brother Arthur, a man obviously as tough as his late brother, arrived in Newton to kill Anderson. But the Texan had been wounded in the gunfight and had gone back home. It took Arthur McCluskey two years to find his man but he eventually ran him to earth in Medicine Lodge, Kansas, a haven for buffalo hunters and other tough characters.

James Grahame was present when they agreed to a duel to the

death, Arthur McCluskey generously giving Anderson a better
sporting chance than his brother had received at the Texan's
hands.

Grahame was interviewed by a reporter from a Missouri newspaper called the *Republican* some fifteen years after the fight. He
still remembered every vivid, bloody detail.

'It was agreed that they should fight to the finish with six-
shooters and bowie knives,' Grahame told the reporter. 'The
spectators ranged in two lines with a sufficient space in between
and the desperadoes stood back to back. At a word, each walked
ten steps and turned. Then they began firing. Twelve shots in all
were fired and only two failed to tell. The spectators could see
the men waver as each ball struck them, and then with curses
and taunts at the bad marksmanship of the other, each would
stagger forward, firing as they came. When the pistols were
empty, the bowie knives were taken.

'The men engaged in a hand to hand fight. They were too
weak to stand long and were soon on their knees, fighting and
with both hands. It was no stage combat, no posing, but all
work. They swore and cursed and bit. They hardly paused. Each
was too eager to kill the other to waste time in anything but
cutting. The blades were in their throats, their sides, near the
heart. The men literally weltered in blood.

'The hardened spectators turned away, asking if the death of
one or the other would not soon end the struggle. At last, Mc-
Cluskey, too weak to longer evade or strike, received Anderson's
knife in the neck. The jugular was severed and he fell forward,
dead. Anderson had just strength enough left to crawl triumph-
antly upon him and he too, fell, and in a moment, had expired.
That was a game fight.'

Grahame had arrived in the United States after adventuring in
various parts of the world. He was 41 years old when interviewed
and gave the reporter a detailed account of his travels.

'In 1864, while still a boy, he went to New Zealand, being
attracted there by the wonderful description of the place given by
a Captain Jenkins, who brought a delegation of Maori chiefs to
England,' said the journalist. 'He became overseer of a sheep
ranch, and after a year, joined those, who, under the gold excitement, went to Hoki Taka. While there, he was hurt by a land-

slide and was taken to Australia for treatment. He was in Melbourne at the time the steamer bearing the gifted Gustavus E. Brooke, sank on its passage to that place. After some years spent in the wars with the bush rangers, young Grahame came to America and at once went to Texas. His New Zealand and Australian training disposed him to the pursuits of the trappers, and for years, he followed that life on the border.'

After his job with the Texas Pacific came to an end Grahame worked as a scout for the United States Army. At one time he was based at Fort Griffin and while there may have run into a fellow countryman who was serving with the Army.

This was Jack Masterson – no relation to 'Bat', Ed and Jim Masterson, lawmen in Dodge City, Kansas – who had seen a great deal of action as a virtual soldier of fortune. Masterson had fought in a British Army regiment in the Crimea and had then emigrated to the United States. He had fought with the French forces in Mexico who were trying to keep Emperor Maximillian, an Austrian arch duke, on the throne there. Later he joined the Confederate Army towards the tail end of the Civil War and when they surrendered he joined the United States Army. In the early 1870s he was a Quartermaster sergeant at Fort Griffin and was a silent partner in Sam Stinson's general merchandising store.

Edgar Rye, old time justice of the peace in the wild town on The Flats, a tough section at the foot of the hill on which Fort Griffin stood, was Masterson's friend and used to tell the following tale.

One morning Masterson was visiting Sam Stinson and had left his horse on a lasso outside the store. One 'Snaky Jim' cut the lasso and rode away on the horse.

Rye quoted Masterson as saying: 'Well, I call that a scurvy trick to take a sneaking advantage of a gentleman when his back is turned – especially when it will be difficult to explain to the Colonel how I came to lose one of the best cavalry horses in the service.'

What he really said was probably far more colourful. And he got a reprimand to boot.

Over in Mason County, Texas, in 1875 there was a little 'war' going on between the Texan cattlemen and the German immigrant farmers. There was a revenge side to it, as the leader of the Texans was exacting his own brand of justice for the murder of his cattleman friend.

And right smack in the thick of things was an Englishman, Major Henry M. Holmes, a former Union officer who had established a law practice in Mason. He was the local correspondent for the San Antonio *Herald* and his detailed despatches to them must have got him into a great deal of danger from both feuding parties. A lot of men got killed on both sides before the Texas Rangers managed to put a stop to things. Major Holmes was lucky not to have been one of them.

Little 'wars' and local feuds like the one in Mason were not uncommon in the early West – especially in post-Civil War Texas. Billy the Kid was active in one of the bigger 'wars' – in Lincoln County, New Mexico, in 1878. There was another big one in Pleasant Valley, Arizona, a decade later.

But the biggest and best organised was the Johnson County War in Wyoming in 1894. This had broken out when the big cattlemen sought to drive out the small farmers (if you believe the farmers' story); or because the small farmers were stealing the big cattlemen's beef (if you believe the cattlemen's version). Either way, it was a big war with hired gunfighters imported from Texas by the cattlemen.

An Englishman named Harry Wallace, about whom absolutely nothing else, unfortunately, is known, went along with the band of gunfighters to see the fun. And for some strange reason he took along his violin – possibly he had nowhere to leave it. The gunmen killed two small farmers – who, they alleged, were the leaders of the cattle rustlers – and were subsequently besieged themselves in the old TA Ranch not far from Cheyenne, Wyoming. The beseigers were the small farmers assisted by their friend the Sheriff and an itinerant preacher who had nothing better to do that day. Upwards of two thousand shots were fired at the Ranch and the defenders might well have been killed to a man but for the timely arrival of a troop of the Tenth (Coloured) United States Cavalry.

And throughout the seige, so the defenders reported afterwards, the Englishman Harry Wallace stood on a table playing stirring airs on his violin to keep up their spirits.

The cattlemen's gunfighters were arrested and charged but in due course were released after political strings had been pulled. But before this, they had their photograph taken, a group picture in fact. And there, standing at the back – minus violin – looking like the last man on earth to have such deeds of valour attributed to him, is Harry Wallace.

After the charges were dropped the participants returned to whence they came. And as no one knew where Harry Wallace came from, no one knew where he went.

It was in Cheyenne, Wyoming, that an Englishman from Falmouth, Cornwall, learned not to interfere with other people's wives.

The Cheyenne *Democratic Leader* of 18th July, 1884, told his sad tale under the headline 'Bound To A Horse's Back'.

'When Mr Boussaud reached his ranch about the middle of June, he found the cowboys nursing a young man whom they had rescued from the back of a bronco,' the paper said. 'When discovered, the modern Mazeppa was lashed to the horse, entirely naked and unconscious. The animal was about broken down, as if from long running, and was easily lassoed by the cowboys, who cut the thongs and released the strange captive.

'This happened about two weeks before Mr Boussaud's arrival and during all that time the stranger had lain in a stupor. A few days before Boussaud left on his return journey to Omaha, Nebraska, having a little smattering of medical knowledge, he succeeded in restoring the patient to consciousness and his recovery was rapid.

'When able to talk he said his name was Henry Burbank, that he was an Englishman, and 34 years of age. About three years ago at Falmouth, England, he formed a partnership with a friend named Thomas Wilson, some years his senior, and with him came to America to embark in the cattle business. They cast around for a while and finally settled in northwestern Nebraska, where the range was unlimited and herders few and far apart. They built a comfortable little ranch on a little stream, where Wilson's young wife reigned as housekeeper, attended by two or three domestics.

'Burbank was a handsome young gallant, and while Wilson was absent riding about the range found it agreeable to make love to the latter's wife. This went on for some months, until in the latter part of May one of the cowboys who had a grievance against Burbank surprised him and Mrs Wilson in a compromising situation and informed the woman's husband, whose jealousy had already been aroused. That night Burbank was captured, while asleep in bed, by Wilson and three of his men, and bound before he had a chance to resist. Wilson had him stripped of every bit of clothing and bound on the back of a wild bronco, which was started off by a vigorous lashing.

'Before morning Burbank became unconscious, and is therefore unable to tell anything about his terrible trip. He thinks that the outrage was committed on the night of May 27 and he was rescued on June 3, which would make seven days that he had been travelling about the plains on the horse's back without food or drink and exposed to the sun and wind. Wilson's ranch is about two hundred miles from the spot where Burbank was found, but it is hardly probable that the bronco took a direct course and therefore must have covered many more miles in his wild journey.

'When fully restored to health Burbank proposes to make a visit of retaliation on Wilson and will be backed by Boussaud's men and also a squad from the Ogalalla (sic) Land & Cattle Company whose range is near Boussaud's.'

Nothing more was reported by the local Press so perhaps Mr Burbank thought better of the matter. He may even have returned to Falmouth a much wiser man.

Another Englishman who had to learn the hard way was William Lewis. Only the way he learned was harder than Burbank's way.

Lewis had a 160-acre homestead in Wyoming and boasted that he had stocked his rangeland with cattle he had stolen from his neighbour John C. Coble, boss of the Iron Mountain Cattle Company. After remonstrations to desist had been ignored, Coble served notice on Lewis to quit the country. Lewis served notice on Coble that he had better travel armed in future.

This was too much for Coble who imported Tom Horn, an old friend, who had established a reputation in closed circles for being a hired gun.

In August, 1895, George Shanton, a neighbour of William

Lewis, came across the Englishman's bloody corpse. Dr Rohr-
bough, the Laramie County Coroner, noted that Lewis had been
shot three times from a distance of about three hundred yards
and that the weapon used was probably a .44 calibre rifle.

The outcome of the affair was quite satisfactory to everyone
but Lewis. The Iron Mountain Cattle Company lost no more
stock; Lewis's neighbours were not troubled by his noted
hostility; Tom Horn was not charged with the killing.

But, speaking of the assassination several years later, Horn
remarked with a laugh: 'He was the worst scairt son of a bitch
you ever saw.'

Horn was hanged in 1903 for a murder he probably did not
commit.

Jimmy Mercer, an English cowboy down in Arizona got shot
at too. But he was more fortunate: his would be assassin missed.
It happened the year before Lewis got killed and the marksman,
oddly enough, had once been friends with Tom Horn. But this
had been some years before when Horn, before he went bad, had
been a scout and interpreter at the San Carlos Apache Indian
Agency. His sharpshooting friend was an Indian known as the
Apache Kid and he was Sergeant of Apache Scouts. But this was
before the Kid went bad too.

Kid's real name was Has-kay-bay-nay-tayl which meant Brave-
and-tall-and-will-come-to-a-mysterious-end. After he went bad
he waged a one-man war on the white population of Arizona.

They still laugh down around the camp fires on the Arizona
ranges when someone tells the story of Englishman Jimmy
Mercer and his brush with the Apache Kid.

In February, 1894, Mercer was camping near Oracle, Arizona,
with his friend Ed Clark. Some five years before, William Diehl,
a partner of Clark's, had been killed by the Apache Kid and
Clark had sworn vengeance. An old-time scout who really knew
Indians, Clark had served with the Wallapai Scouts and had
acquired that nickname. He and his new partner, John Scanlon,
were in Tucson when Jimmy Mercer met up with the Apache
Kid.

Mercer was taking a bath in a creek when his dog pricked up
its ears. Mercer looked around to see who was coming and at
that second a gun roared and a bullet sent up a little waterspout

at his side. Mercer leapt from the stream and, leaving his trousers on the bank, did a hundred yards dash for his cabin unencumbered by running shorts or shoes.

He barred the door, borrowed a pair of Clark's trousers which were much too big, took up a rifle and prepared to stand off the whole Apache nation if needs be.

Mercer was still there when 'Wallapai' Clark returned and the old scout guessed that the marksman was the Apache Kid. That night he shot at two Indians, killed one and thought he wounded the other. In the morning they found the dead Indian was a woman. The Apache Kid always travelled with a squaw and to his dying day – in 1928 – 'Wallapai' Clark believed that he had avenged his partner William Diehl by killing the Kid's squaw and probably fatally wounding the Kid as well.

Either way, the death of the Apache Kid has never been satisfactorily explained.

His name was prophetic. For he was brave; he was tall (for an Apache); and he did come to a mysterious end.

Over the territorial line, in New Mexico, some fifteen years before Jimmy Mercer set up his record for the hundred yards 'free-style', a young English nobleman was trying his hand at ranching – and making some pretty silly mistakes, much to the good-natured amusement of his neighbours who had undertaken to help him learn the business.

Young Lord Trayner had just come down from Cambridge when his father suggested that he try to make his mark in the United States. This seemed like good advice, so with the promise of an allowance every three months, Lord Trayner set out. He wound up in New Mexico and, as luck would have it, fell in with the Jones brothers who were the first Anglo family to settle in Lincoln County.

The Jones Boys – Bruce, Henry, Nib, Frank, John, Sam, Tom, Bill and Jim – knew cattle and knew New Mexico. Lord Trayner could not have gone to better teachers. They sold him a ranch, a number of horses, a wagon and other equipment. At their suggestion he bought a brand and some cattle. Bruce, the youngest of the boys, went to work for him.

Trayner talked a lot about ranching but did little of it. He built new quarters on to the ranch. He liked Bruce Jones and

Bruce liked him. The only thing Bruce did not like was that Trayner called him 'Chappie'. He liked it a lot less when the cowboys began calling him 'Chappie' too.

There came a parting of the ways when Trayner sent to Corpus Christi, Texas, for a dress suit. Bruce asked if his lordship intended to wear it.

'Got it for you, Chappie,' Lord Trayner told his foreman. 'Going to promote you and raise your wages. No more outside work for you. This is for you to wear when you serve dinner.'

Bruce Jones was on his horse and headed for home before his startled employer could even ask him why. And he never went back.

Then his lordship built a wine cellar and this became the talk of the Pecos country. A wagon came from Corpus Christi laden with bottles and Lord Trayner had them put on the shelves of his cellar. Word got around that he was going to open a saloon.

Soon afterwards he went to Corpus Christi himself and when he came back he had with him an English lady he had met there and married. Lady Trayner had brought with her some beautiful china and she showed it to her new-found women friends. Each plate, she told them when pressed, was worth about $25. This caused more talk than the wine cellar. For $25 would buy a good cow and a calf.

Then Lord Trayner started drinking; not just drinking like everybody else in Lincoln County; he was really drinking. After that his remittance money went faster. Soon he was selling off his cows; then his horses; his men quit when they could not collect their wages; he sold some of Lady Trayner's jewellery; then her $25 plates – Sam Jones bought nine of them for $5.

One day Sam was riding past the Trayner place and saw that the wagon was gone. The house looked deserted too. When he investigated he found they had just upped and left – gone back to England so he heard later.

'Even so,' he used to say, 'they'd lasted longer than I expected – mighty nigh two years.'

Lady Trayner's life must have been sad as she saw first her husband's then her own money disappearing down his throat.

Cabin of William McGaa in Denver in 1858. This was the first cabin built in what would become the capital of the State of Colorado. Painting by Dudley Judson shows McGaa standing in the doorway. *(State Historical Society of Colorado.)*

William 'Denver' McGaa, the first child born in Denver. Son of William Mc-Gaa and his Cheyenne wife. *(From Smiley's 'History of Denver', 1901 – State Historical Society of Colorado.)*

Cheyenne wife of William McGaa in 1874. *(From Smiley's 'History of Denver', 1901 – State Historical Society of Colorado.)*

To face page 30]

William Smith, Marshal of Wichita.
(*Kansas State Historical Society.*)

'Bloody Bill' Anderson, Missouri Guerrilla.
(*State Historical Society of Missouri.*)

Jim Bridger, who quoted Shakespeare
in the wilderness. (*State Historical
Society of Colorado.*)

Thomas Dimsdale, Montana Vigilante
leader. (*Historical Society of Montana.*)

If she had been made of sterner stuff she might have been able to take her wastrel husband in hand. Over in Hillsboro, New Mexico, not too far from the Trayner place as the crow flies, a little London girl named Sadie Orchard was getting along all right in much tougher circumstances.

Tales of whores with hearts of gold are legion. They are also, usually, legendary. But two London girls, one part-Negro and the other an East End Cockney, have left behind them authenticated stories of whoring and hearts of gold in widely separated times and parts of the West.

Sadie Orchard – that was her married name, her maiden name is now forgotten – arrived in the wild and rugged town of Hillsboro at the height of its gold boom. New Mexico in 1886 was a far call from her native Stepney but the desires of men were pretty much the same.

Eighteen-year-old Sadie, who prided herself on her tiny size and especially her tiny feet, became a whore. Pretty soon she had amassed enough money from the free-spending miners to set up a 'house' and employ other girls. Sadie's business boomed and in due course she achieved a mantle of respectability by marrying J. W. Orchard, a colourless individual who had never had two cents to rub together.

Together they established, at Sadie's instigation, the Lake Valley, Hillsboro and Kingston Stage and Express Line. They bought – or rather Sadie did – two Concord coaches and a stage wagon and went into business. Meanwhile Sadie kept her 'house' and saw to it that its occupants were well cared for. Initially the stage line had been established to give J. W. Orchard something to occupy him. But soon Sadie found that he was letting business slip and she knew the time had come for her to take an active interest in the company.

Whenever there was a new 'call' that gold had been found all business houses lost their employees as the hopefuls rushed to the scene of the strike. Sadie Orchard's stage line was no exception and stage drivers flocked to each call along with all the rest.

Soon Sadie began to drive the coaches and eventually she made the daily run from Hillsboro to Kingston.

She was to boast in later years: 'Neither of my coaches was ever held up while I was driving.'

B

An unauthenticated but persistent story of Sadie has it that on one occasion, while driving through a narrow gorge, some reservation Indians who had somewhere got some liquor decided to stop the coach Sadie was driving. They were not dangerous, just bent on a little fun.

Sadie, so the story goes, climbed slowly down from her seat, bull whip in hand. And as she reached the ground she began to lay about her with it flattening all the Indians within range.

After that the reservation bucks left her coaches well alone.

Kingston, terminus of the stage line, had a population of five thousand, twenty-two saloons, three dance halls, several general stores – and no church. It was Sadie, in the first flush of semi-respectability as the proprietress of a legitimate business, who started the drive to build a Protestant church and by the time she had finished collecting from the pimps, gamblers and whores she knew so well there was $1,500 in the hat.

In Hillsboro, her home town, Sadie established a successful hotel to which came practically all New Mexico's top politicians of the day. Even more than her stage line, the hotel gave Sadie the respectability she craved. She affected stylish dresses and drank imported wines. When she had the time she went for long rides, riding sidesaddle and decked out as she believed an English lady of quality should be dressed.

Hillsboro in time played out; Sadie moved to Kingston; The stage business collapsed; J. W. Orchard drifted away; Sadie established a 'house' in Kingston. She was forty-six years old at the outbreak of the First World War, a wealthy little woman who ran a bordello in a New Mexico mining community. Three years later America entered the war and Sadie's business dropped off as the menfolk left for the front lines.

Now Sadie really came into her own.

During the big influenza epidemic Sadie nursed the sick and often laid out the dead. She supported the family of a man serving time in prison because during prosperous bachelor days he had been a good customer at her 'house'. Many families who were in need were helped over difficult periods through her generosity.

Today the once-thriving Kingston is a ghost town except for the handful of tenacious old-timers who still reside in it. The church that Sadie collected for is gone but the big stones it was built from can be seen in the walls of the few houses still lived in. They have been 'remodelled'. One of her Concord coaches is on display in the Museum of New Mexico in Santa Fe.

Sadie Orchard died in 1940 at the age of seventy-two and the few people who still remember her all agree that 'in spite of everything, Sadie was a real lady'.

More than thirty years before Sadie Orchard crossed the Atlantic another London girl was dispensing similar joys, and amassing an even larger fortune, in far off Nevada.

Julia Bulette was born in London in 1832. Her mother was English, her father of mixed Negro-white parentage, was from New Orleans. And that is about all that is known of Miss Bulette's early life. She set sail for America at the age of twenty-one and arrived penniless in New Orleans, her father's home town.

Julia went to work as a 'hostess' in a plush gambling establishment in the French Quarter but within months a yellow fever epidemic sent her, along with hundreds of others, fleeing from the city. She went far, to San Francisco, in fact, and re-established herself in her chosen profession.

In the autumn of 1859 the dark-eyed beauty packed her bags once more. This time she went to Virginia City, Nevada, where silver fortunes were being made and lost overnight. Virginia City was rough, tough and expensive. Flour sold for $1 a pound, whisky for $1 a drink and eggs for $10 a dozen. From Julia's point of view conditions were even better: she was the first of her profession to arrive in town.

In time, she was to make Virginia City her own. And Virginia City, or, at least the male population, was to take her to its heart.

Her first friend was a young reporter on the Virginia City *Territorial Enterprise* named Samuel Clemens. He too would become famous in his time – under the pen-name of Mark Twain.

Clemens introduced her to Henry Comstock, after whom the fabulous silver strikes known as the Comstock Lode were named; to John MacKay, soon to be the richest man in America and founder of the Postal Telegraph; to George Hearst, later to found America's biggest newspaper empire; to Marcus Daly, future copper king of Montana. All were captivated.

By the time spring came and the passes across the Sierras were open again Julia Bulette had earned enough money to open a 'house'. The first stage in from California brought girls. Julia's monopoly was ended. So to prevent competition she hired the girls for her 'house'. In time she built a new 'house' which became famous as 'Julia's Place'. Everything was the best: the furnishings, the food, the liquor – and especially the girls. It cost her a quarter of a million dollars.

On 4th July, 1861, Julia Bulette was made an official member of the Virginia City Engine Company No. 1, the city fire brigade. It was a signal honour.

During the great mine disasters and the even greater fires Julia Bulette transformed 'Julia's Place' from its normal calling and turned it into a hospital. Many a pioneer woman, her husband killed in a mine cave-in, had her fare back East paid by Julia Bulette. Those widows who stayed could always rely on her support until they established their own independence or married again.

The Civil War split Virginia City into pro-Union and pro-Confederate camps. Old friends became enemies overnight. Julia was staunchly pro-Union, as were the fire companies. There were gunfights on the streets in the name of the war. But all men forgot their political differences and put away their guns when they visited 'Julia's Place'.

After the war Virginia City continued to boom. And the fame and fortune of Julia Bulette boomed with it.

Then, 11.30 a.m. on the morning of Sunday, 19th January, 1867, one of Julia's girls, not hearing her moving around, knocked on her door and went in.

Julia Bulette lay on the floor her head covered in blood. She had been battered and strangled to death.

Her murder outraged Virginia City and was reported in newspapers across the entire West. But it was not until April that her murderer, John Millain was arrested.

Julia's funeral had been the biggest Virginia City had ever seen. The trial of her killer set another record, so did his public hanging on 24th April, 1868.

Today, the only regularly tended grave in the old weed-strewn Virginia City cemetery – which is no longer used – belongs to the little London girl who did so much for the town she loved and which loved her.

CHAPTER TWO

THE WRITERS

IN THE wake of George Frederick Ruxton, whose book of travels
entitled *Life in the Far West*, published in 1849, had created an
extraordinary interest in the American West, came a flood of
travellers eager to see 'The Wild West' – and to write about it.

These English travellers, most of them well-to-do upper-
middle-class people – along with a sprinkling of titled gentry –
noted down everything they saw. They had an unfortunate
tendency to compare the wild, unsettled frontier with their more
peaceful homeland but their writings, however critical, show
the West pretty much as it was in the last three decades of the
nineteenth century.

Mrs F. D. Bridges began a world tour in 1878, passed through
India and much of south-east Asia the following year and
reached the American West in the summer of 1880.

Alighting from a train at the tough silver boom town of Leadville, Colorado, she was amazed to find a gun-toting hotel tout
who loudly yelled: 'If any man says the Clarendon ain't a first-
class house, I'll put a bullet through him!'

Mrs Bridges wisely stayed at the Clarendon and told about
it in her book *Journal of a Lady's Travels Round the World*
which was published in 1883.

Colon South reported in his book *Out West; or, from London
to Salt Lake City and Back*, published in 1884, that he had been
offered every possible amenity in a hotel in a small Wyoming
town.

He was informed he would find 'Baths, gas, hot and cold water,
laundry, telegraph, restaurant, fire alarm, bar-room, billiard
table, daily papers, coupé, sewing machine, grand piano, a clergy-
man, and all other modern conveniences in every room.'

No mention was made of a bed, but there was one there as well.

There were other 'modern conveniences' also to be had at
this establishment.

South reported that he was told that he could have 'Meals
every minute if desired, consequently no second table . . . Waiters
of every nationality and colour desired. Washing allowed in
rooms, and ladies giving an order to "put me on a flat iron," will
be put one on at any hour of the day or night.' There were
still other services. 'A discreet waiter, who belongs to the
Masons, Oddfellows, Knights of Pythias, and who was never
known to tell even the time of day, has been employed to carry
milk punches and hot toddies to ladies' rooms in the evening . . .
The office clerk has been carefully selected to please everybody,
and can lead in prayer, play draw poker, match worsteds at the
village store, shake for drinks at any hour, day or night, play
billiards, good waltzer, and can dance the German, make a
fourth at euchre, amuse the children, repeat the Beecher trial
from memory, is a good judge of horses, as a railway and steam-
boat reference is far superior to Appleton's or anybody else's
guide, will flirt with any young lady, and not mind being cut
dead when "pa comes down".' It was promised, that 'the proprietor will take personal affront if any guest on leaving should
fail to dispute the bill, tell him he is a swindler, the house a
barn, the table wretched, the wines vile, and that he – the guest
– was never so imposed upon in his life, will never stop there
again, and means to warn his friends!'

The Englishman's dress, normal at home, was pretty bizarre
by Western standards. John J. Fox wrote that when he arrived
in Cheyenne, Wyoming, in 1885 wearing a brown bowler hat, a
white collar, English riding breeches and leggings he attracted
much attention but no comradeship. He rapidly bought a pair
of cowboy boots, a cavalry hat, overalls and a blue flannel shirt.

'After the change the men where I boarded were not only
approachable but friendly,' he said.

But regardless of comfort or otherwise in hotels, apparel or
railway trains the English man or woman visiting the West for
the first time wanted to see two things: Indians and the fabled
'Wild West' of which they had heard so much.

William Hepworth Dixon found Denver, capital of Colorado,
as wild as any could want it. He was there in 1866 and in his

book *New America*, published the following year, he wrote: 'As you wander about these hot and dirty streets, you seem to be walking in a city of demons. Every fifth house appears to be a bar, a whisky-shop, a lager-beer saloon; every tenth house appears to be either a brothel or a gaming-house; very often both in one. In these horrible dens a man's life is of no more worth than a dog's.'

Rough and rugged Leadville, Colorado, where detractors of the Clarendon Hotel were promised a hasty demise, was visited by a number of English travellers. Mrs Bridges saw a notice which said pointedly: 'All Chinamen will be shot.'

Walter Gore Marshall found the boom camp rather less than wild. He wrote of it in his book *Through America; or, Nine Months in the United States*, which was published in 1881. He had seen in the town two years earlier, he wrote, four daily newspapers, five churches, three schools, one hundred and ten saloons and a branch of the Y.W.C.A.

The Reverend Foster Zincke, vicar of Wherstead, added to the Englishman's conception of the 'Wild West' in his book *Last Winter in the United States* which was published in 1868.

'Every man in the West goes always armed,' he wrote. 'And it is one of the most imperative laws of Western society, that, if a man insults you in any way, you are bound to then and there shoot him dead. Society requires you to do it, and if you do not, you will be shot yourself; for the man who has insulted you, supposing that you can only be waiting for an opportunity, will think it better to be beforehand with you.'

Roger S. Pocock had an exciting adventure to relate in his book *Following the Frontier* which was published in 1903. He had travelled in the West in the 1880s and wrote that in Montana: 'I came into a community of outlaws who live by robbing trains, banks, coaches, and trading-posts, by stealing bunches of cattle and shooting sheriffs – they had shot one six weeks ago.'

It was the Indians who fascinated the Englishmen, schooled as they were on the 'noble red men' of James Fenimore Cooper's *The Last of the Mohicans, The Deerslayer* and others.

Maria Theresa Longworth, pen name of the Viscountess of Avonmore, was horrified by the Indians she saw at a railway station in Wyoming. In her book *Teresina in America*, which was

published in 1875, she wrote that they had 'besieged the doors
and windows [of the railway carriages], and were wildly im-
portunate for white bread and cakes'. They had, she remarked
sadly, descended to 'the lowest degradation to which humanity
can descend.'

Sir Charles Wentworth Dilke, son of the proprietor of the
Athenaeum quoted a typical Westerner's attitude to the Indians.
He recorded it in his book *Greater Britain: A Record of Travel
in English-Speaking Counties During* 1866 *and* 1867 which was
published in 1872.

'We can destroy them by the laws of war, or thin 'em out by
whisky; but the thinning process is plaguey slow,' the man told
him laconically.

The Westerners wanted the Indians exterminated. The East-
erners wanted them protected and shown the benefits of civilization.

Hepworth Dixon summed up the muddled thinking of contemporary Eastern and Western Americans when he wrote in
1867: 'The Eastern cities are all for rose-water and baby-talk;
the Western cities are all for revolvers and bowie-knives. Each
section has its sentiment and its passion. In Boston no one believes a red Indian can do wrong; in Denver no one believes a red
Indian can do right.'

The English writers found the West fascinating. But peers
and commoners alike usually ended up with the conclusion that
there was no place quite like England – and they were glad to
get back home.

Lady Mary Rhodes Carbutt, who wrote *Five Months' Fine
Weather in Canada, Western U.S., and Mexico* which was published in 1889, found America a dirty place where the food was
bad and the accommodation worse.

Lady Rose Pender wrote in much the same vein in her book
A Lady's Experience in the Wild West in 1883 which appeared
six years later.

The same year Sir Henry Edwards published his *Two Months'
Tour in Canada and the United States in the Autumn of* 1889.

Lady Theodora Guest, sister of the Duke of Westminster,
visited the United States on the spur of the moment due to the
fact that the 'hunting [season] came to its last sad day even

earlier than usual'. Her book *A Round Trip in North America*
appeared in 1895, her trip having been brief and to the point,
fitted in between the end of the 'hunting' season and the beginning of the 'hot weather'.

Sir Lepel Henry Griffin's book *The Great Republic*, which
came out in 1884, was written for political reasons. He was
writing critically of the United States, he explained, not to upset
the Americans – though it had this effect – but to sound a warning to England about the pitfalls of democracy in the hands of
the common people. He was particularly against the 'surrender
[of] political power into the hands of the uneducated masses'.

Rudyard Kipling toured the United States in 1889 and 1892.
His book, *From Sea to Sea; Letters of Travel*, came out in two
volumes ten years after his first trip across the West.

Sir Edwin Arnold, editor-in-chief of the *Daily Telegraph*
passed quickly across the West on his world tour. His despatches
appeared in his paper and were later expanded into a book entitled *Seas and Lands* which was published in 1891.

A journalistic traveller of lesser eminence was William Fraser
Rae who made the overland trip by rail on behalf of the *Daily
News* in 1869 and wrote of his trip under the title *Westward by
Rail: The New Route to the East* (meaning the Orient), the
following year.

George Warrington Stevens called his book *The Land of the
Dollar* and it came out in 1897. The year before he had been sent
to the United States by the *Daily Mail* to cover the Presidential
elections.

Sir Alfred Maurice Low, who visited the West for the *Morning Post* wrote one of the best English-authored books on the
Western states. It was called *America at Home* and appeared in
1905 at a time when he was chief correspondent in America for
his paper, a job he held for nearly half a century.

Sir William Howard Russell, who covered the Civil War for
a number of newspapers, put together a two volume work called
Herperothen; Notes From the West which appeared in 1882.

The Lord Chief Justice of England, Charles Russell Russell,
who was later to preside at the trial of the Jameson Raiders and
to mediate in the boundary dispute between Venezuela and
British Guiana, visited the West as a young man. His diary

account of his travels came out in 1910 under the title *Diary of a Visit to the United States of America in the Year* 1883.

To the English traveller the West was to be seen and often wondered at. But home was home and he was glad to get back to it.

CHAPTER THREE

THE FIGHTERS

THE BATTLE OF ADOBE WALLS – Texas, 27th June,
1874

Dodge City businessman A. C. Myers was in his office when
the messenger arrived. He stumped in and handed Myers a letter.

'Dear Myers,' it read. 'We have been attacked by Indians and
corralled since June 27th. The attack was made early in the
morning and the battle lasted about three hours.

'I have put the place in a state of siege. If you can, get an
escort of fifty men. Indians are in sight all the time. We are well
armed and can stand off 500 Indians. There are 200 of them.
We were completely taken by surprise.

'All the men are of the opinion that the Indians are waiting
for reinforcements and will then give us another battle, but we
are fixed for them.'

The letter was signed by Fred Leonard, the young Englishman who was Myers's partner in the trading store they had
established at Adobe Walls, a small settlement in the heart of
hostile Comanche country.

The men at Adobe Walls were outnumbered ten to one by the
most determined and warlike tribes in Texas. They had been
under siege for four days when Fred Leonard wrote to Myers
and handed the letter to a daring messenger who had volunteered
to try to slip through the Indian lines to summon help.

But even then Fred Leonard's stiff-upper-lip Britishness was
apparently unperturbed.

Myers re-read the letter – 'if you can, get an escort of fifty
men'.

An hour later a relief column rode south from Dodge City.

The Comanches, Kiowas and Southern Cheyennes had been
active during the first few months of 1874. The camps of buffalo

42

hunters had been attacked, their horses killed and their hides burned. Individual hunters had been captured on the plains and tortured to death. The little settlement at Adobe Walls had grown up around a store established by Myers and Leonard and had soon become the headquarters for the buffalo hunters. An Irishman named Tom O'Keefe had started a blacksmith shop and another Irishman, Jim Hanrahan, had opened a saloon. Then German-born Charlie Rath set up a restaurant and store.

The Comanches several times came within sight of Adobe Walls but did not dare to attack until a young medicine man arose among them who could, he claimed, make the white man's bullets harmless. His name was Isa-tai and he alone had received from the Great Spirit a formula for a paint which would turn away bullets.

The Comanches and Kiowas watched the white men encroaching upon their traditional hunting grounds. They had seen the slaughter of the great shambling buffalo which provided them with meat, clothing, thread and fuel. They had seen other game killed wantonly or driven away.

By the middle of 1874 they were ready for an all-out war. A young warrior was chosen to lead them. Ultimately he would become the most powerful Comanche on the plains. He was Quanah – Quanah Parker to the white men – son of a Comanche war chief and a captured white girl named Cynthia Ann Parker.

The combination of Quanah Parker as a warchief and Iso-tai as a medicine man was enough to ensure that the summer of 1874 would see bloody fighting in Texas.

On 26th June twenty-eight men and one woman went to bed at Adobe Walls supremely conscious that the Indians might attack at any time within the next few days. Word had been received that an Englishman named 'Antelope Jack' Holmes and his German partner, 'Blue Billy', had been murdered by the Indians some fifteen miles from the settlement.

Soon after dawn on 27th June, Billy Dixon, one of the top hunters on the plains, looked up from saddling his horse to see the hills around Adobe Walls dotted with Indians. Horrified, he watched as more and more came into view until several hundred painted Comanche, Kiowa and Southern Cheyenne warriors were ranged on the slopes around the settlement.

Yelling a warning, Dixon dashed for Hanrahan's saloon where he had left his guns.

In the saloon were Jim Hanrahan; an Irishman named Oscar Shepherd; 'Bat' Masterson, the youngest man in the camp and the one destined to become the most famous as a fast-shooting frontier marshal; and five other hunters.

In Rath's store and restaurant were Tom O'Keefe; a fellow-Irishman named James Langton; five other men; and Mrs William Olds, the only woman in the settlement.

Meanwhile Fred Leonard was turning his store into a fort. Sacks of flour were piled at the windows, heavy furniture was dragged across the doorway and ammunition was passed out. In the store were Leonard, an Englishman named Harry Armitage, a tough Scots hunter, Jim Campbell, and eight other men.

The screaming Indians swept down on the settlement and sent their plunging ponies weaving in and out of the buildings, firing as they rode. The big buffalo guns of the hunters roared back at them and three warriors toppled from their horses. Two brothers named Shadler, who were caught in their wagon outside the settlement, were shot down by the Indians and scalped.

Then the Indians made a second attack. Again they were driven back. And again they attacked. By midday the Indians had suffered heavy losses in killed and wounded and had temporarily retired beyond rifle range.

Fred Leonard told the men in his store to watch for an attack while he ran to the stable to see that his horses were all right. It was a foolhardy venture but he slipped out through the door and sprinted across the open ground. Billy Tyler, a young hunter, followed him.

The Comanches attacked at once.

Leonard, realising that he could not reach the stable, dodged back. Tyler followed him, running low for the store. The door opened and Leonard leapt inside. Tyler turned in the doorway to fire at a painted warrior. A dozen Comanche bullets ripped into him and he collapsed. The hunters dragged him in but he was dying.

'Bat' Masterson ran from Hanrahan's saloon and headed for Leonard's store. He leapt inside and kneeled beside Tyler. They had been partners and Masterson was almost in tears as he watched the life ebbing out of his friend.

Tyler begged for water but there was none.

Masterson straightened, picked up a bucket and headed for the door. But 'Old Man' Keeler grabbed it from him and rushed out. Bullets tracked him to the well and whistled round his ears as he drew a bucket of water. He ran back, miraculously unscathed, and Tyler had his drink before he died.

The Indians had been using a bugler – a deserter from the Tenth Cavalry – to direct their attacks but he made the mistake of showing himself once too often. Fred Leonard and Harry Armitage pulled down on him and fired. They both missed. He leapt up and ran but Armitage's second shot sent him sprawling.

Late in the afternoon a buffalo hunter named Henry Lease volunteered to try to slip through the Indian lines and get help from Dodge City. He rode out after dark and headed north.

The following day the Indians attacked again. Once more they were repulsed and a stray bullet, most of its force spent, hit Quanah Parker and flung him from his horse with a dislocated shoulder. He was out of action for the rest of the fight.

Isa-tai, the medicine man, and his bullet-proof paint were already discredited. He tried to regain his prestige by pointing out that Quanah had been hit by a bullet and had survived. But the final blow for him came when a shot from one of the buffalo hunters killed his horse which he had also painted with his concoction.

Later in the day Billy Dixon killed an Indian on a hillside with an incredible long shot from his buffalo gun. The hunters measured it later and found the distance to be 1,538 yards – only a little less than a mile.

The fight had gone out of the Indians but they continued to besiege the settlement. Other hunters slipped through the ring to join the defenders. Several who tried were killed. Billy Olds, husband of the restaurant cook, was killed when his gun went off accidentally as he was descending a ladder. He was the last casualty.

On 1st July, the fourth day of the siege at Adobe Walls, another messenger slipped away and headed for Dodge City carrying Fred Leonard's letter to his partner.

The relief column which rode south was seen by the Indians who fled back to their camp. Twenty-eight buffalo hunters had been too much for them. Now there were more than seventy.

The Battle of Adobe Walls was over.

'About 25 or 30 Indians were killed – we found eleven,' Fred Leonard said later. 'I killed one Indian that I know of, and don't know how many more, as I was shooting at them with my revolver from forty to sixty yards for twenty shots.

'I took one scalp. Fred Myers killed two Indians; they rode around and up to the corral and got off their horses, and fought as brave as any man I ever saw. We had 150 Indians around our place at one time.'

THE BATTLE OF THE LITTLE BIG HORN – *Montana, 25th June, 1876*

Lieutenant Colonel (brevet Major General) George Armstrong Custer watched proudly as the twelve Troops of his beloved Seventh Cavalry passed before him in review as they marched out of Fort Abraham Lincoln to begin an expedition against the hostile Sioux Indians.

He watched as a Gatling gun detachment from the Twentieth Infantry, two Companies of the Sixth Infantry and one Company of the Seventeenth Infantry followed the fighting Seventh out of the main gate. The eight hundred men, three quarters of them made up by the Seventh, represented the biggest military campaign ever mounted against the Sioux and Cheyennes.

Custer smarted under the restrictive order which had placed him under the command of General Alfred H. Terry. It had been his own fault and he knew it, but it did not make the humiliation any less stinging. He had criticised President Grant and his personal and official family while testifying before a Congressional Committee and had been deprived of his command. Only after repeated urging by senior officers had he been permitted to accompany the expedition at all, even in a subordinate capacity. He knew that only a big victory over the Indians could restore his prestige and possibly save the military career that he loved. The public would acclaim him a victor – it was America's Centennial Year – and the President would be unable to withstand the pressures which would be put upon him.

There were a lot of troops in the field that summer of 1876. General George Crook had marched out of Fort Fetterman, Wyoming, with several hundred troops in March and part of the force had attacked and routed a camp of Cheyennes the same month. They had failed to snatch a resounding victory, but it had been a beginning. By the summer Crook was again in the field and the Seventh Cavalry joined in the campaign against the Indians.

The troops reached the Powder River and General Terry divided the Seventh Cavalry. The right wing, commanded by Custer, marched along the south bank of the Yellowstone River to the mouth of Rosebud Creek. Meanwhile, Major Marcus A. Reno and the rest of the Seventh rode south to scout for hostiles near the headwaters of the Powder and Tongue Rivers. In the valley of the Rosebud they found a fresh Indian trail leading towards the valley of the Little Bighorn River.

Reno led his command onwards to join up with the rest of the Seventh at the mouth of the Rosebud. He did not know that while his scouts were examining the fresh trail, General Crook, only forty miles away, was fighting for his life against a strong force of Sioux under Crazy Horse, the great Sioux leader. Crook was forced to retreat and go into temporary camp. But the officers of the Seventh knew nothing of this on the night of 21st June when they discussed the plan of campaign on board the steamer *Far West*.

Custer mapped out a plan and it was agreed upon.

General Terry and Colonel John Gibbon would march up the Bighorn River and enter the Little Bighorn Valley from the north. Custer and the rest of the troops would enter the valley from the South and the Sioux would be crushed between the two forces.

They rode out the next morning, travelling light and relying on the pack train to keep them in supplies while they were in the field. On 23rd June they struck the Indian trail and followed it all day. They covered twenty-eight miles the following day before Custer called a halt. He planned to rest in the hills on the 25th June, wait for Terry and Gibbon to reach the valley from the north, and attack on the following day. The halt was only temporary and the troops wearily climbed back into their saddles and rode on. They reached the hills and went into camp at 2 a.m.

Before first light Lieutenant Charles A. Varnum, Chief of the Crow and Arikara scouts, rode out with 'Lonesome' Charley

Reynolds, one of the toughest and most respected of the old scouts on the plains. Soon after dawn they looked down into the valley which led to the Little Bighorn and saw the dust stirred up by the ponies of a tremendous Indian encampment which stretched for several miles along the banks of the river.

It was the biggest assembly of Indians ever gathered on the plains, some fifteen thousand Sioux and Cheyennes. Three thousand of them were warriors, the cream of the fighting men of the two Indian nations. Hunkpapa Sioux under the command of Gall and Crow King had joined with Inkpaduta's band of Yanktonnais and Santees. The Minneconjou Sioux were led by Lame Deer and Hump. Two Moons, the Northern Cheyenne leader, had brought in his people to join Crazy Horse and his Oglala Sioux.

Custer had no way of knowing the size of the Indian encampment. His scouts said it was very large but he disbelieved their estimates. He was a day ahead of Lieutenant Low and the detachment of Gatling guns and Gibbon's infantry. But he knew that the Indians would soon discover the presence of the troops. And he knew that an overwhelming victory would reinstate him in the President's favour.

Swiftly he called his Troop commanders together and detailed them off with precision.

Captain Frederick H. Benteen, commander of Troop H, was put in charge of Troops D and K as well, told off as the first battalion and sent riding away towards a line of low hills some two miles distant.

Major Reno was put in command of the second battalion, made up of Troops M, A and G, and sent to ride down the south side of the creek leading towards the Little Bighorn. Varnum's Indian scouts went with them.

Captain Thomas McDougall and Troop B were ordered to bring up the rear and guard the pack train.

As Reno's battalion rode away Custer detailed the other commanders to follow him and led off down the right bank of the creek parallel to Reno. Strung out behind him were Troop C, commanded by Captain Thomas W. Custer, his brother; Troop E, commanded by Lieutenant Algernon E. Smith; Troop F, under Captain George W. Yates; Troop I, commanded by Captain Miles W. Keogh, an Irish soldier of fortune who had once been a member of the Papal Guards at the Vatican; and Troop L, commanded by Lieutenant James Calhoun, brother-in-law of Custer. A civilian, Mark Kellogg, special correspondent of the *Bismark Tribune*, fell in behind them.

They made up a combined body of two hundred and thirty-one men. Reno's battalion, marching on the other side of the creek, numbered one hundred and twelve.

Ten miles further on they encountered a band of forty Indians riding hell for leather towards the Little Bighorn. Custer sent an order to Reno to follow them with the second battalion. He moved out at a fast trot and disappeared. Soon a messenger returned to Custer with the information that the Indians were not running as had been thought; that they were, in fact, preparing to give battle to Reno.

Custer dictated an order to his adjutant, Lieutenant William Cooke, who handed it to Italian-born trumpeter Giovanni Martini. He raced off to find Benteen who was somewhere in the rear.

It read: 'Benteen: Come on. Big village. Be Quick. Bring Packs. W. W. Cooke. P.S. Bring Pacs.'

Reno had already found a band of Indians and had charged their position only to find his troops hopelessly outnumbered. He withdrew to a ridge and tried to fight them off. 'Lonesome' Charlie Reynolds was killed and soon afterwards Custer's favourite Arikara scout, Bloody Knife, received a bullet in his head. Two officers were killed and then Reno retreated across the river and forted up once more. The surgeon and his orderly were killed and the battle raged on. By mid-afternoon Benteen and his command arrived and drove off the Indians for long enough to enable him to reach Reno and swell the numbers of embattled troops.

But nobody knew what had happened to Custer. He had last been seen riding off into the Bighorn Valley and Trumpeter Martini had been the last man to see him alive.

Precisely what happened in the last hours when the five Troops of the Seventh Cavalry made their desperate last stand can only be pieced together from the positions in which the bodies were found and from the conflicting testimony of Indians who were in the battle and told their stories later.

For there were no survivors.

A few minutes after Trumpeter Martini raced off with his message to Benteen the Troops clashed with a band of Hunkpapas under Gall. They fought their way to a hogsback ridge which ran parallel to the river and attempted to hold it.

But the Indians came in overwhelming numbers.

Gall's forces assaulted the ridge from the south and Crazy Horse led his Oglalas up the north face. The Seventh spread out along the hogsback, managing to keep more or less together by Troops.

Crazy Horse hurled his warriors against Captain Yates' Troop F and Captain Keogh's Troop I who were covering the others. He was joined by the Cheyennes under Two Moons.

Sergeant Frederick Nursey of Troop F went down. He died a long way from his native Suffolk. Trooper Felix James Pitter, who came from Aylesbury, died with Troop I. Edward W. Lloyd from Gloucester and John Parker from Birmingham died soon afterwards with Troop I.

Stragglers broke away from the battle and worked their way up towards the north end of the ridge. It was to become the gathering point for the last men of the doomed Seventh.

Soon after Troops F and I had been destroyed, Crazy Horse led his warriors to join Gall who was poised to smash Lieutenant Calhoun and Troop L on the southern tip of the ridge.

Trooper William B. Crisfield probably never had time to think of his native Kent as he fought the Indians until they killed him. Trooper Henry Roberts, a Londoner, fell soon afterwards. James J. Galvan of Liverpool went down near Farrier William H. Heath from Staffordshire.

Meanwhile, Captain Tom Custer's Troop C was fighting for its life in a ravine between the ridge and the river. Lieutenant Algernon E. Smith and Troop E were fighting a little further up the ravine.

The Sioux under Lame White Man swept up the ravine and overwhelmed Troop C. Trooper Frederick E. Allen, of Milton, went under. Nearby Jeremiah Shea, a Londoner, died beside his friend James Hathersall of Liverpool. The Sioux poured on by and destroyed Troop E. Trooper Herod T. Liddiard of London was killed alongside Trooper John S. Hiley from Rugby. Corporal Thomas Hagan of Lancashire died near them.

By now all five Troops of the Seventh had been virtually destroyed.

A small number of survivors from the various Troops managed to struggle up to the northern point of the ridge where Custer was preparing to fight the massed strength of the Indians.

They shot their horses and arranged them in a rough circle to form barricades. They laid out what ammunition they had left and as the Indians came along the ridge shells were levered into rifle chambers. Some of the Springfield carbines had jammed and sweaty hands gripped them to be used as clubs.

Lieutenant Colonel Custer made a final check that his two English Webley Bulldog pistols were loaded and gave the order to fire.

It was all over by four o'clock in the afternoon. Custer's Last Stand had passed into history.

Reno and Benteen with the remnants of Troops A, D, G, H, K and M remained under siege for the rest of the day. That night they could see the camp-fires of the Indians and hear the throb of drums.

The Indians attacked soon after dawn and kept the troops pinned down all day. Twice Benteen ordered his men out of the hastily-dug rifle pits and sent them charging against the Sioux who broke and fled.

On one of those sorties a small band of troops, led by Trooper James Pym from Oxford and Trooper Jonathan Robert from Surrey, dashed right through the Indian lines, filled camp kettles with water from the river and managed to rejoin their comrades as they withdrew to the rifle pits. The water was not enough to go around and was doled out to the wounded in Dr H. R. Porter's field hospital. Pym and Robert were both awarded the Congressional Medal of Honour – the American equivalent of the Victoria Cross – for their bravery.

Later in the afternoon of 26th June the Indians began to slip away. But, fearing a trap, Reno and Benteen held their ground. The following morning there were still fewer Indians and they moved off when a column of troops rode into view. It was Gibbon's Seventh Infantry and some men of the Second Cavalry.

Lieutenant James H. Bradley, in charge of Gibbon's Indian Scouts, rode up to report counting one hundred and ninety-seven bodies on the hills where Custer had fought and died.

Reno and Benteen gathered their tired troops together and the remnants of the Seventh Cavalry rode away from the Little Big-horn Valley.

On 6th July, 1876 – eleven days after the Battle of the Little Bighorn – a telegram was handed to the editor of the New York *Herald*. He unfolded it and read: 'General Custer attacked the Indians June 25, and he, with every officer and man in five companies were killed. Reno with seven companies fought in entrenched position three days. The *Bismark Tribune's* special correspondent was with the expedition and was killed.'

It was the first news of Custer's Last Stand.

Historians have been arguing about it ever since.

CHAPTER FOUR

THE LAUGH-GIVERS

TO THE West the Englishman, especially the high-born one, was a source of almost endless fun. Frequently the Englishmen the Westerners met were either wealthy travellers or prosperous young noblemen who came to the West to make their fortunes. The average middle- and working-class Englishman who came as an emigrant was a source of amusement for a while but was soon fully accepted – especially if he conformed to the American way of life.

Sometimes the English came with the idea that they were superior in some way to the rough, tough frontiersmen and cow-boys who inhabited the Old West. If that was their attitude they suffered for it. Others came cock-sure that they could do every-thing that an American could do and then found that they could not. But to those who came, persevered and stayed the range country extended its traditional warmth and hospitality.

An English milord on a hunting trip was a source of great amusement. John G. Bourke, one of the great soldiers of the plains and great chroniclers of the West, noted one such arrival which caused a stir down in southern Arizona in early 1871.

A man named Speedy, an assistant at the Camp Grant sutler's store, told Bourke and some friends that he had seen a ghost several miles south of the post.

Wrote Bourke: 'As he described it to us, it had much the appearance of a "human", and was mounted on a pretty good specimen of a Sonora plug, and was arrayed in a suit of white canvas, with white helmet, green veil, blue goggles, and red side whiskers. It didn't say a word to my friend, but gave him a de-cidedly cold stare, which was all Speedy cared to wait for before he broke for the brush. A hundred yards or so in rear there was a train of pack mules laden with cot frames, bath-tubs, hat-boxes,

and other trumpery, which may or may not have had something
to do with the ghost in advance. Speedy and his mule were too
agitated to stop to ask questions, and continued into Hermosillo.

'Information received about this time from Sonora reported
that an English "lud" was "roughing it" in and about the Yaqui
country and it is quite possible that he could have given much
information about the apparition had it been asked.'

Such was the travelling equipment of young English noblemen
'roughing it' in the West. But it was not only their travelling
equipment that excited comment, it was also their speech and
their attitude to the Americans.

A cowboy in Dodge City was invited to take a drink by an
English duke on tour. The duke, while paying for the drinks,
found an English coin among the loose change he pulled from
his pocket.

When he had paid for the drinks he showed the coin to the
cowboy.

'You see the likeness of Her Majesty the Queen, on this coin?'
he said. 'Her grandfather made my grandfather a lord.'

The cowboy was very interested. When it came to his turn to
pay for the next round he pulled from his pocket a one cent
piece which had an Indian's head on it.

'See the likeness of that red Injun on this penny?' he said,
passing it across for inspection. 'Well, his grandpappy made an
angel outa my grandpappy.'

In an article entitled 'A Few Mounts' published in the colorado
newspaper *El Anunciador de Trinidad* a cowboy told of an Englishman and his riding prowess on the plains:

'. . . Over in Nevada in '78 came a true born Englishman. He
came, so he informed us, to break horses for a livelihood. The
boys mentioned that probably these horses were different from
those he was accustomed to, and might be harder to break. His
reply was "Mon, a 'oss is a 'oss the world hover, hand h'I've
ridden 'osses after 'ounds and broke many a bad 'un. Besides,
mon, these little fellers aren't big enough to 'ave much strength."
Well, the days passed on and finally Tom got a 'oss to break.
The boys brought him up, and blindfolded him, helped Tom
put on his little pancake saddle and snaffle bit, and held the
"baste" while Tom got on. The blinder was whipped off, and

the 'oss stood braced and still, and then Tom wagged his legs and clucked. Four jumps and a whirl, and Tom was sailing, sailing, sailing. When he came to, and had got the dust out of his mouth, he gave us an account of it all.

' "Why," said he, "the dom baste was nothing like a 'oss. First 'e stood on 'is 'eels, and then 'e stood on 'is 'ead. Then 'e 'umped 'is back like 'e was sick at the stomach, and wanted to puke a bit, and then 'e came down with one of those dirty shakes, 'umped 'is back again and hoff h'I went." '

Another Englishman showed the cowboys that he could ride and they gave him full credit for it. At a rodeo held at Deer Trail, Colorado, to celebrate the Fourth of July, 1869, an Englishman really made good in the contest to win a suit of clothes and the championship. A cowboy who saw this exhibition of riding wrote about it more than thirty years later.

'. . . Emilnie Gardenshire, of the Milliron ranch, was the next rider. Gardenshire let it be known that he wanted the worst animal in the pen, and he got it in the shape of a bay, from the Hashknife ranch, known throughout the section as the Montana Blizzard.

'Gardenshire, rawhide whip in hand, crawled aboard cautiously, and, once firm in his seat, began to larrup the bay unmercifully. A sight followed which tickled the spectators hugely. The Englishman rode with hands free and kept plying his whip constantly. There was a frightful mixup of cowboy and horse, but Gardenshire refused to be unseated. For fifteen minutes the bay bucked, pawed, and jumped from side to side, then, amid cheers, the mighty Blizzard succumbed, and Gardenshire rode him around the circle at a gentle gallop. It was a magnificent piece of horsemanship, and the suit of clothes, together with the title "Champion Bronco Buster of the Plains", went to the lad from the Milliron ranch.'

Stories abound of the Englishmen who came to the cattle ranges and the vast open spaces of the West.

An Englishman new to the West looked across the clear prairie to some mountains which seemed to be only a few miles away, they were so clearly visible. He announced his intention to take a brisk walk to the foothills during the morning and return in time for lunch. The cowboys warned him that the high altitude and the clearness of the air made the mountains seem nearer than they in fact were. They were fully thirty miles away they said. The Englishman would not believe them and set out smartly. In the afternoon two cowboys rode out to see how far the Englishman had got and ten miles from the ranch they found him standing on the edge of a stream taking off his clothes.

He informed them that he was going to swim across the river. They pointed out that the stream was only a few yards wide and a few inches deep.

'Ha!' said the Englishman. 'I know I was fooled by those blasted mountains, but I'll swim this river if it takes me all day.'

The story is told of another Englishman who arranged through an agent to buy a ranch, sight unseen. When he arrived to visit it he was amazed at both the size and the vast herd of cattle grazing out on the prairie.

Turning to the foreman he said: 'By Jove! And where do you find milkmaids for them all?'

The fastidiousness of many of the English amused the rough and ready frontier Americans.

They still tell in the range country about the Englishman who was found sunbaked and blistered on the edge of a clear stream in a dry and arid land. His tongue was swollen through lack of water and as the cowboys rode up he managed to croak a few words.

'My word!' he said. 'Have either of you fellows a tin cup about you?'

The gullibility of the English was also made a butt for jokes. A story told was about the monocled Englishman who arranged to buy a herd of cattle from Senator Stephen W. Dorsey, a sharper-than-usual American rancher. Before the prospective customer arrived the rancher arranged with his cowboys that they would drive the herd round and round a small knoll and between two posts where the Englishman's tally men would be counting.

There was one steer in the herd which was a big, bob-tailed, lop-eared yellow one and had a game leg. The herd was driven between the two posts while the tallymen counted and the Englishman sat with the rancher on their horses near by. Then the herd was taken rapidly out of sight round the knoll and driven back. The old yellow steer came through every time and each time the Englishman watched it with a special interest. Eventually, when the herd – and old yellow – was making its fifteenth trip between the now tiring tallymen the Englishman screwed his monocle tighter into his eye and turned to the rancher.

'There are more bloody, blasted, lop-horned, bob-tailed, yellow crippled brutes than anything else, it seems,' he said reprovingly.

Just for the record, Senator Dorsey later perpetrated a notorious fraud involving Government funds.

There were even Englishmen whose very verbosity could win them battles.

A young Englishman named Vincent arrived in Texas to join his brother who had a ranch on the Panhandle. He prided himself on the number of big words he knew and the cowboys soon realised that they could never win an argument with Vincent because he would start using words they did not understand.

One day a cowhand rode in to tell Vincent's brother, the ranch owner, that there was a squatter on his land. In the era of public land and free grass squatters were common but this one was on privately-owned land and had no right to be there.

Vincent worked up a nice little speech and rode out to deal with the interloper.

'You can't do this thing,' he told the man. 'The land is ours by law, and if you wilfully appropriate it for personal use you will be taking that to which you have no right, and in doing so you will be desecrating every principle for which our ancestors fought and bled.'

And with that he rode away.

The cowboys, who had expected a gunfight or at least a legal action, before the squatter would move, hardly expected Vincent's visit to have altered the situation. But a few days later one of them found the squatter moving off, his wagon loaded with his family and all their belongings.

Curious, the cowboy asked the man why he was leaving without a fight. The squatter told him and the cowboy rode back to the ranch to tell the boys. When they asked the reason the cowboy grinned.

'Oh, he didn't give much reason at all. He said that if Vincent's pappy had fought and bled over that piece of land he kind of figured the kid ought to have it.'

There are scores of humorous stories of the English nobleman, the English dude and the common-or-garden English immigrant on the Plains. But surely one of the best is told in a poem which appeared in the *Denver Evening Post* on 19th July, 1899:

My Lord and the Broncho

He was a fair young Briton, he bore a titled name,
It took two lines of minion, we're told, to print the same;
Clamped in his starboard optic he wore a circle glass,
And used the other looker to see things as they'd pass.
He'd read about the cowboys and Indians and things,
The buffalo that watered at Colorado Springs,
And came out to this country to see the bloomin' show,
And brought his title with him as ballast, don't ye know.

He drifted to a rancho where cattle roam the Plains,
He carried ten umbrellas and quite a bale of canes,
His 'man' marched close behind him, stepped as if built on
     springs,
And carried two port-man-choos stuffed full of lots of things.
The cowboys gazed upon him in wonder most supreme,
And sharply spurred each other to see if 'twere a dream,
And grinned when he addressed them in words drawled beastly
     slow:
'I'm Lord Alphonso Paget De Lawncey, don't ye know.'

He said that as a rider at 'ome he set the pace,
Be'ind the 'ounds he'd ridden in many a frightful chase,
And if 'is 'unter bolted 'e'd teach 'im with the crop
'Twas Lord Alphonso Paget De Lawncey who was up,
He eyed the raw-boned bronchos bunched up in the corral,
And said they were but palfreys, were anything but swell,
And when a bawth he'd taken he'd hawlf a mind to go
And back a beastly creature for a canter, don't ye know.

The Christian cowboys told him it gave them pain to say
Their thoroughbreds were feeding on ranges far away,
But if with condescension he'd back a bronc, they'd choose
A pet that wasn't stylish, but great on the amuse.
They roped a flea-bit cowhorse that seemed 'bout half asleep,
That stood while being saddled as quiet as a sheep,
And when Milord was mounted he said: 'Now let'im go!
'E'd never make a 'unter; too stupid, don't ye know.'

That broncho stood a moment, as mapping out its job,
Then every muscle in it begin to jerk and throb,
An o'er the plain it bounded with wild, excited vaults,
And turned a lot of single and double somersaults!
With tender hands the cowboys bore that astonished lord
From where his titled body had battered up the sward,
And when his wond'ring sense returned he muttered low:
'Such bloody, blasted conduct was beastly, don't ye know!'

CHAPTER FIVE

THE MINERS

THE men and women of Cornwall occupy a unique spot in the story of the opening up of the American West. For while the majority of the English, Welsh, Scots and Irish immigrants were engaged in ranching, Indian fighting, serving in the Army and store-owning, the Cornish were labouring in the bowels of the earth as miners, one of the traditional occupations of their native country.

When the great silver, tin, and lead mines were being opened up, particularly in Colorado, there was a cry for genuine, hard-rock miners to work them. The native American miners were used to little more than the coal and copper mines of Michigan and the eastern seaboard states. Hard-rock mining and the peculiar skills and feats of human endurance that it required was not completely above their capabilities, but it taxed them to a degree and was unpopular because of it.

There were Cornish miners in the copper mines of Michigan and many of them answered the call for hard-rock miners in Colorado. They began arriving there in the late 'sixties, grew to a flood in the 'seventies and 'eighties and then tailed off to a trickle which only completely dried up around 1910.

Ernest Morris, who arrived in Central City, Colorado, in 1890 found that 'the majority of the population was Cornish'.

Their latent wit, intelligence, sense of fun, ignorance of many things, capacity for practical jokes, superstitions, love of singing and strange use of the English language marked them down as 'different' and the Americans were not slow to make them the butt for their jokes. But at the same time they liked and respected them for their skill as miners and their friendliness – once an outsider could penetrate their clannishness and reticence.

The Cornish miners worked well in the mines and satisfied foremen and managers were always anxious to take them on.

Often when a job fell vacant the Cornish miners would be asked if they knew a fellow countryman who would like to fill it. A much inter-related people, the Cornish often knew of a cousin or relative still in Cornwall who would like to emigrate to the United States and they would refer to their Cousin Jack who would like the job. Sometimes they had a friend who would like the job but felt he would stand a better chance if referred to as a relative rather than a friend. The name Jack was – and still is – popular among them and soon the Americans began to hear so much of Cousin Jack that they applied the name to all Cornish-men.

Later, when they began to send for their wives and families the women became Cousin Jennies to the Americans, possibly – but by no means certainly – because the big male donkeys used in the mines were called Jacks and the female donkeys were known as Jennies.

The Cornish brought their own cooking to their new homes and saffron cake, starrey-gaze pie and, in particular, pasties became commonplace in the mining camps of the Old West. No self-respecting Cousin Jack would think of going on shift at the mine without his pasty in his lunchbox.

And they brought with them words almost as old as the Cornish mining industry but which to the Americans were new. Words like stope, lode, stull and sprag got into the language and stayed there to become part of the jargon of the mining industry to this day.

Because of the clannishness, superstition and, to the Americans, strange linguistic traits, the Cornish became set aside and conspicuous in the mining communities in which they settled.

They liked to call people 'my 'andsome', 'my son' and 'my beautay' and this, along with their habit of dropping the letter 'h' where it should have been and adding it where it did not belong, made them the butt of many jokes. At first the jokes were told in derision but in time the good-natured Cornish accepted them and they grew into part of the folk lore of the new country.

The Cornish did well in most fields they tried. Mining was their first love but they soon became mine owners, store keepers, cowboys and even deputy sheriffs.

'Bloody Franky' Broad, a Cornishman, was one of the toughest deputies who ever rode out of Tombstone, Arizona, under the famed and feared Sheriff John Slaughter of Cochise County. In his spare time 'Bloody Franky' either worked in the deep silver mines around which Tombstone had grown or staged wrestling matches for money.

Today all the first generation Cousin Jacks are gone. So are most of the second generation ones. But third and fourth generation are absorbed into almost every mountain community in the modern-day West. They still retain their independence, their national pride and their sense of humour, but to a great extent the clannishness is gone.

Gone too are most of the inimitable Cousin Jack stories which became so much a part of the humour and folk lore of the mining West in the last forty years of the nineteenth century. Various scholars have managed to preserve some of the stories in the journals of historical societies and in obscure privately printed collections but many have been forgotten and so lost altogether. Many of the funniest were about sex, but their very coarseness precluded their publication in staid journals and today they are only heard if told by some ribald old hard-rock miner with a long and retentive memory.

Colorado had been especially fortunate, not only in absorbing so many Cornish but in finding a dozen or so dedicated collectors who had tramped the hills visiting the few long-time residents of the old mining camps, talking with them and getting them to remember their stories. Most of the Cousin Jack stories which have found their way into print have come from Mountain City, Central City, Nevadaville, Russell Gulch or Black Hawk in Colorado. But many of them, although having been collected there, were also current in other parts of the West.

These are just a few of them:

A Cousin Jack, noticing the large amount of lunch that a new miner put away, remarked: 'My 'andsome, I would rather keep thee a week than a fortnight.'

* * *

An illiterate Cousin Jack received a letter from his girl-friend in Cornwall. He took it to an American miner friend and asked

'Poker Alice' Tubbs, Queen of the Western Gamblers. (*Dr J. Leonard Jenniwen.*)

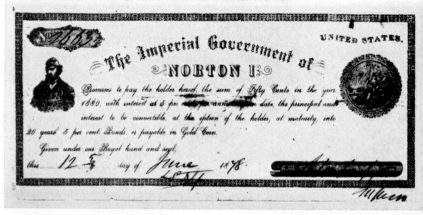

Scrip issued by 'Emperor' Norton. (*Wells, Fargo Bank History Room.*)

John H. Tunstall. (*Courtesy Maurice Garland Fulton.*)

Frank Collison, Yorkshire-born cowboy (*Panhandle — Plains Historical Society.*)

him to read it. But he stood behind the man, holding his fingers over the man's ears so that his partner could not hear the contents of the private letter.

* * *

A very prosperous Cousin Jack in Nevadaville was approached to make a donation for a new chandelier for the Methodist Chapel.

'Sure h'I'll gie thee fifty dollars,' he said. 'But 'ho's goin' to play it?'

* * *

A Cousin Jack working at the Pewabic mine on a cold day told the hoistman to heat up his pasty before he came up for lunch, meaning the man to put it beside the boiler. When he came up at lunchtime his pasty was gone and the hoistman said he ate it.

'Goddam 'ee,' said the Cousin Jack. 'I didn't mean fer 'ee to eat 'im up, but to 'eat 'im up.'

* * *

A Cousin Jack went to the railway station at Central City to meet a newly-arrived fellow countryman. As they drove down Spring Street into Main Street the newcomer looked up at the initials I.O.O.F. on the Odd Fellows Building and remarked: 'Don't look no bloody 'undred feet 'igh to me.'

* * *

A Cousin Jack went to see a show at the Opera House in Central City and a particularly attractive girl made a big hit with the audience. Amid the rapturous applause a man at the back began shouting, 'Encore! Encore!'

The Cousin Jack turned to him and grunted: 'To 'ell with encore. Let's 'ave the same girl back again.'

* * *

A Cousin Jack called for jury duty was closely questioned by the defence lawyer who demanded to know if he was prejudiced against the prisoner and if he felt that he could give the man a fair trial.

c

'Yes, my son, I can,' replied the Cousin Jack. 'I always come to a case with this thought in my 'ead: if 'e idn't guilty, wot's 'e 'ere for?'

* * *

A Cousin Jack presented himself at a mine, told the manager that he was an experienced miner and was given a job. He was put to work with an old miner who had worked for years without an accident. The miners' method was to work in a two-man team, one man holding the metal drill and turning it, the other man striking it with the sledge hammer. After the old Cousin Jack had taken a turn at striking, the new one took his place. His first strike missed the drill and struck the old miner's arm, breaking it.

The new man was then put with another miner and soon the same thing happened. He was put with a third miner and repeated the previous two incidents. The enraged manager sent for him and told him that he was a poor excuse for a miner. He did not know how to strike and had proved this by breaking the arms of three of the best men in the mine.

'What have you got to say for yourself?' the manager demanded.

'They bloody old arms is rotten,' growled back the Cousin Jack.

* * *

Another Cousin Jack who did not like hard work was paired off with a fellow countryman. They worked for a while, the lazy Cousin Jack holding and turning the drill, the other one doing the striking. After about half an hour the one doing the striking was exhausted. Sweat was pouring off him and he was blowing hard. Still the lazy Cousin Jack made no effort to relieve him of the sledge hammer.

Snapped the tired Cousin Jack: 'Thee've got good wind for turning.'

* * *

After a mining accident which sent a Cousin Jack to hospital two of his countrymen met. One asked the other how badly their friend had been injured.

'Aw, 'e wasn't 'urted worth a dom; 'e only 'ad one eye blowed out,' said the Cousin Jack.

* * *

A Cousin Jack who was working a small mine of his own sent some rock specimens to the local assay office for a report. They came back far below his expectations. The Cousin Jack had worked hard in the mine in the hope of striking rich grade ore and he was very disappointed. He moaned to his friends and implied that the man in the assay office was a swindler who was only saying that the mine was worthless in the hope that the Cousin Jack would sell at a low price.

' 'Ere, my son,' one of his friends told him. 'Thee shouldn't talk that way about 'im, 'e's a good man. What'll thee do when thee meets 'im in 'eaven?'

' 'Eaven?' the dissatisfied Cousin Jack snapped back. 'If I do meet 'im in 'eaven, I shall pick up a rock and bust the bloody wing of 'im.'

* * *

A Cousin Jack won a duck at a fair and took it home to put with his chickens. Feed, like everything else, was scarce and costly in the mining regions and when he saw the duck waddling along shovelling up about three times as much food as the chickens the Cousin Jack picked up a stick and hit the duck with it.

'Peck for peck, my beautay, no shovellin' goes on 'ere,' he said.

* * *

A Cousin Jack, who helped his wife run a boarding house, went into a saloon one day and noticed a stuffed owl on a shelf above the bar.

' 'Ere, my son, 'ow much for that broad faced chicken up there?' he asked.

'That ain't no broad faced chicken,' said the barman. 'That's a howl.'

'I don't care 'ow hould 'e is, 'e's good enough for boarders,' said the Cousin Jack.

* * *

An illiterate Cousin Jack who had struck it rich bought himself a large gold watch with a heavy chain and wore it around town, even though he could not tell the time. An American, who knew of the Cousin Jack's limitations, decided to play a joke on him and, pointing to the watch, asked what time it was.

The Cousin Jack pulled out the watch and showed the face of it to the miner.

'There 'tis,' he said. 'Thee wouldn't believe *me*.'

* * *

Two Cousin Jacks were on a mine face drilling. The rope which was anchoring them to pegs hammered into the sheer face of the wall broke and one of them fell to the bottom of the tunnel. The drill however stayed in the hole they had been drilling and the other Cousin Jack grabbed it and held on. Eventually he had to let go and dropped to the bottom where his friend was waiting.

'Dammee,' said the friend. 'I knew thee was slow, but I didn't think it would take thee five minutes to fall twenty-five feet.'

* * *

A Cousin Jack who was working a notably unsuccessful mine was asked by a friend how it was going and how the ore was.

'Where 'tis, there 'tis. Where 'tisn't, there I am,' he replied.

* * *

One of the Cousin Jack superstitions was that if the candle in the mine fell off the wall or went out three times for no apparent reason it meant someone was at home making a pass with the Cousin Jack's wife. One Cousin Jack, whose candle had gone out three times, rushed home without bothering to change out of his heavy mining boots. He dashed inside and finding a man in his house, the Cousin Jack rolled up his sleeves and prepared to fight.

But the romantic caller refused to fight.

'This ain't no fair ketch,' he said. 'Thee has boots on.'

* * *

Up in Montana a labour leader named Marcus Daly was responsible for the introduction of Irish labourers into the mines and from the beginning the Cornish fought them at every chance. In Virginia City there were full scale riots and even killings. Two Irishmen were hanged and a number of Cornishmen and Irishmen went to the penitentiary for causing damage to persons and property during the clashes.

After Cornish/Irish troubles at the Parrot Mine in Butte the Cousin Jacks were fired.

As they walked down the hill from the mine for the last time one stopped and looked back.

'Goodbye, thee bloody birdie, the beastly Irish have thee now,' he said bitterly.

*　　*　　*

When miners were drilling it was not uncommon for the drill to strike a fissure in the rock. It had to be worked loose and left a three-cornered hole which was difficult to re-drill. The Cousin Jacks called a fissure a 'fitchure'.

One, when asked by the foreman why he and his mate had stopped work, replied: 'Dammee, bloody 'ole fitchured.'

*　　*　　*

One winter's day four Cousin Jacks decided to ride over to a near-by mine to see a friend on their day off. They went to the local livery stable and asked for a horse. One of them added: 'Gi'e us long-backed bugger.' The liveryman asked why the horse must have a long back. 'Four of we is goin' to ride,' said the Cousin Jack.

Later the stage coach passed the four Cornishmen sitting forlornly on the horse which was stuck in a snowdrift. The driver asked if there was anything he could do.

'No,' called out one of the Cousin Jacks. 'We's bloody 'orse fitchured.'

*　　*　　*

Some mines allowed the miners to lease a shaft or a section of the workings and pay for it by producing extra ore from the company's part. Then, in their spare time, they were free to work their leased sections. The Cousin Jacks called this 'tributing'.

When the superintendent of one mine put an end to 'tributing' at his mine the Cousin Jacks were enraged.

They gathered in a saloon to drown their sorrows. One of them was a lay preacher and the others asked him if he could say a prayer that might help them to get their 'tributes' back.

The lay preacher began: 'Dear Lord, does Thee know Simon 'arris, superintendent of the Poor Man Mine? If Thee know 'im, we wish for Thee to take 'im and put 'im in 'ell and there let the bugger frizzle and fry until 'e give us back we tributes. And when 'e do, dear Lord, we ask Thee to take 'im out of 'ell again, and grease 'im up a bit, and turn 'im loose, Amen.'

*   *   *

They are all gone now, that sturdy breed of men who crossed an ocean and half a continent to burrow like moles in the bowels of the earth. Their bones lie in the graveyards of Central City, Butte, Virginia City, Nevadaville, Goldfield, Russell Gulch, Pioche, Eureka, Austin, Bannock, Rawhide, Bodie, Aurora and half a hundred other now-forgotten mining camps scattered across the West.

CHAPTER SIX

THE COLONISERS

STRUNG out across the Kansas prairie were a score of huntsmen in traditional pink. Fox hounds bayed as they took up the scent of a coyote. Hours later the huntsmen returned, tired but happy.

The Runnymede Hunt had had a good day out.

Runnymede, Kansas, is no more. A lone grave marks the site of the strangest, wealthiest and drinkingest town in Kansas. The actual town site, once the home of some two hundred English immigrants, is a wheatfield.

The town was the dreamchild of an Ulster Irishman named Francis J. S. (Ned) Turnley who paid £800 for three square miles of fertile land in the Chikaskia River bottom north of the town of Harper. Turnley, instead of ranching his land, hit upon a get-rich-quick scheme which gave birth to a town and brought to Harper County the strangest set of immigrants Kansas ever saw.

For Turnley advertised in *The Times* and *The Spectator* offering to teach young gentlemen the art and science of cattle ranching and promising at the end of the 'course', to help them find and purchase ranches of their own.

Several dozen wealthy Englishmen immediately made arrangements to emigrate to Turnley's new town of Runnymede. And a number of British peers with errant sons decided that the town offered just what they were looking for, providing a chance to get rid of the sons and educate them at the same time – and all this for a mere £500.

Major Charles Seton, fresh from service with the British Army in India, resigned his Commission and joined a party of sixteen English men and women who sailed on the Red Star Line's crack ship *Britannic* on 29th May, 1889. They arrived at New Orleans and travelled to Houston, Texas, for the last leg of their journey.

'So anxious was I to find agreeable quarters at the end of my journey that, with fearful extravagance, I sent a long cablegram to Turnley to build me a house forthwith and have it ready for me upon my arrival,' Major Seton, a man of considerable private means, wrote years later. 'When I reached Runnymede there was no house in sight, and we were glad, likewise disgusted, to find lodging at the ranch house, where we braved the terrors of corn bread and fat bacon – a new shock to our digestive apparatus – until houses were built.'

Seton's wife joined him in September, 1889, and a stream of immigrants followed during the next two years. The little town grew until it covered seven city blocks and sported some of the most elegant homes in Kansas.

'Some of us had considerable money – enough to be considered poor in England but comfortable in the United States,' recalled Major Seton. 'None of us had any financial sense. While we waited for a miracle to be performed, that would transform our arid home into a blooming garden, and the town of Runnymede into a vast metropolis, we feasted and danced and made merry.'

Fine thoroughbred horses and a pack of foxhounds were imported; a race track with steeplechase jumps was laid out; a three-storey hotel, the biggest in Harper County, was built.

There were only two things missing in the town; young women of marriageable age and liquor. The women never came and Kansas, being, technically, a prohibition state, forbade the selling of liquor.

Such restrictions, however, were ignored by the citizens of Harper, the county seat, some twelve miles from Runnymede, and it was there that thirsty English throats were slaked.

Wrote Seton: 'One guileless father thought that Runnymede would be the salvation of his son, who had acquired a big thirst for liquor. The lad kept the trail hot between Runnymede and Harper, and maintained an irrigation plant that would have overwhelmed the children of Israel. He always had some kind of a jug.'

Prohibition was a failure in Runnymede. For, when the Englishmen tired of the twelve-mile ride to Harper, they imported their drink by the trainload from Chicago.

'One youth fell heir to £500 a year, and the thermometer in

Runnymede went up several degrees. What a time he had!' recalled Seton.

The citizens of Harper got plenty of amusement out of their English neighbours. They laughed at their fine blooded horses, which were no match for the tough little American cow ponies; the 'pancake' saddles they used, which were so unlike the big Western saddles; and most of all at their dress.

'The men imagined they were in the very heart of the West, where the blood ran wild and reddest,' wrote Seton. 'They wore cowboy outfits, and an arsenal of guns and knives rattled on them as they walked. They would not go outside the house unless armed to the teeth. They were fond of posing for their portraits in photograph galleries in Harper and Wichita, and I tremble even now at the terrible desperadoes that gaze at me from the faded pictures. Captain [M.] Faulkness was an especially fierce-looking "cowboy", and was almost afraid of himself when in full regalia.'

Steeplechase racing was held every fortnight and citizens from Harper came to watch the fun. The Englishmen dressed up for the occasion and provided plenty of amusement.

'The riders bedecked themselves in all the glory of Solomon,' wrote Seton. 'John Lobb was the beau of the steeplechase. Upon one occasion he appeared wearing a white, stiff-bosomed shirt, a collar and a flowing necktie, a black alpaca coat, checked trousers that reached half-way to his knees, white socks, dancing pumps, a granger hat and lavender kid gloves. He was a poor rider, could barely keep his seat, and at the finish his head was thrown back at an angle of forty-five degrees, while his legs were around his horse's neck.

'Dick Watmough, who affected cowboy hats and a ferocious-looking buffalo overcoat, ran this race with red-and-white bunting wrapped around his legs, hatless, and wearing a black shirt.'

G. S. John Lobb was only in Runnymede for a short time. He arrived in early 1889, and returned to England the same November. His brother, Leslie Manderson Lobb, had been in the town since May, 1887, but it was John that Seton recalled so vividly: 'Who can forget him?' he commented.

Dick Watmough, the other colourfully-dressed rider, was Richard W. Watmough, Lord Watmough, who arrived at Runnymede in November, 1888. He ran a meat market and dealt in fine livestock until he died in May, 1890.

Dr and Mrs A. H. Fraser arrived in November, 1889; three months earlier Mr and Mrs F. E. Fryer and their young son had arrived to start a livery stable; Major Smirthwaite of Scarborough arrived to start a ranch; C. W. Sturgis, arrived in August, 1889, but went home again six months later to join the British Army; Captain Percy Woods arrived with Sturgis and stayed on to start a blacksmith shop; five brothers, Bredin, Hooper, Hope, Wade and Way Hancock, also arrived in 1889.

Runnymede had its new arrivals; it had its marriages; and it had its deaths.

Herbert L. Way had barely arrived in Runnymede before he sent for his fiancée, Kittie Kitching. She came on 17th July, 1890, and they were married the next day.

Captain and Mrs Thomas Sharp Hudson arrived in early January, 1890, with their children, Tom and Pinkie. By the end of the month the captain had died. Vernon Elliott Slack came to Harper County in April, 1887, and began a livery stable. His brother arrived two years later bringing their mother to take over the stable after brother Vernon had died.

Runnymede also had a prize fight to enliven things.

An Irishman named Paddy Shea lived at Wichita and was the heavyweight boxing champion of Kansas. A bout was arranged between Shea and one of the young English gentlemen and the champion knocked out his opponent within two rounds.

When he came round the loser handed Shea a gold watch and a sheaf of paper money with the words: 'You're a blooming good lad, don't you know.'

At least, that is what Kansas tradition says he said.

Runnymede grew until it had a population of nearly two hundred. Then came the crash. The Kansas, Mexico and Orient Railroad – part of a grandiose scheme to build a railway from Kansas City to Acapulco, Mexico – failed to pass through Runnymede and was built two miles south.

Ned Turnley, the town's founding father, gathered up his wife, two sisters-in-law and secretary and sailed back to Ireland much richer than he had been five years before.

The Englishmen began to drift away. Some went home; others

went West. The hotel was put on wheels and dragged away to Alva, Indian Territory. At least six of the Runnymede colonists served as officers during the Boer War.

There is nothing left of the town now. Nothing except the lonely grave of Captain Thomas Sharp Hudson, a simple marble shaft surrounded by a sagging fence of monumental iron.

'Runnymede was a combination of British inexperience, credulity, some money, considerable cockneyism,' recalled Captain Charles Seton who stayed on in America. 'It withered like a flower and died. Its citizens are scattered from ocean to ocean.

'A few years wore off the varnish, broke the bank and turned out the lights. But Rome howled in the interval.'

BOOK TWO

CHAPTER SEVEN

THE HUNTER

IN THE summer of 1854 the city of St Louis was electrified by the arrival of an enormous wagon train complete with forty professional guides and a genuine British baronet.

Drawn up in the main square were twenty-one two-horse charettes – commonly called Red River carts – one hundred and twelve head of horses, three milk cows, eighteen oxen, four six-mule wagons, two three-yoke wagons – and a brass bedstead.

The owner of the brass bedstead and the reason for the enormous hunting party was Sir George Gore, eighth baronet, of Manor Gore, County Donegal, Ireland.

Sir George in a deer-stalker hat and Norfolk jacket strolled about the camp, his ginger side-whiskers carefully brushed and perfumed. The quintessence of the 'huntin', shootin' and fishin' ' aristocracy, he was born in Brighton, Sussex, in 1811, the only son of Sir Ralph Gore and Lady Grace Maxwell. He was educated at Winchester School and Oriol College, Oxford, and succeeded to his father's Irish title at the age of thirty-one, in 1842.

He had hunted in Africa and Asia and in 1854 decided to equip a hunting party for the Western territories of America. From his house in Brighton he made up a list of what he would need. At Mound City, Missouri, he bought the equipment and hired guides. He filled a wagon with firearms, including seventy-five large bore hunting rifles, among them guns by Purdy, Westly, Richards and Joe Manton, as his private arsenal. His personal valet accompanied him. So did a man brought especially from Ireland to tie the flies when Sir George went fishing.

Sir George's personal accommodation consisted of a green and white striped tent ten feet by eighteen feet, complete with carpet. He took along his brass bedstead and canopy, for Sir

George did not believe in uncomfortable travel. For wet weather, when the pitching of the tent would have been inconvenient, a spring wagon had been converted to make comfortable living quarters. Solid silver drinking cups embossed with the family coat of arms were kept in a locked box whose key was held by the valet. To complete the personal effects were a carved marble washstand, an iron dining table and a large wooden bathtub.

In May, 1854, he was ready to leave St Louis for the West. His chief guide was Henry Chatillon, an experienced frontiersman who knew the Rocky Mountains as well as any man living at the time.

Captain Randolph B. Marcy, who had fought Indians and explored the country Gore was to travel through, wrote: 'The outfit and adventures of this titled Nimrod, conducted as they were on a most gigantic scale, probably exceeded anything of the kind ever before attempted on this continent.'

Passing through Leavenworth, Kansas, the hunting party was seen by a small boy named William Frederick Cody who was to become famous in his own right as hunter, scout, showman and friend of royalty under the name of 'Buffalo Bill'.

Sir George's great friend Sir William Thomas Spencer Wentworth-Fitzwilliam, sixth Earl of Fitzwilliam, began the journey with him. Sir William had been Member of Parliament for Malton (1837–41 and 1846–47) and was M.P. for Wicklow (1847–51). At this time he was serving as Lord Lieutenant of the West Riding of Yorkshire (1853–92) and Aide-de-Camp to Queen Victoria (1884–94). But in 1854 he was just a wealthy young nobleman on holiday taking a leisurely trip round the world with his telescope. For Sir William was a keen amateur astronomer.

The hunting party reached Fort Laramie, Wyoming, in June and their passing was noted by the correspondent for the *Daily Ohio State Journal* at Columbus who sent a report to his newspaper which was published on 24th June.

'Between forty and fifty dogs, mostly greyhounds and staghounds, of the most beautiful breeds, compose this part of the expedition,' said the newspaper. 'He had a large carriage, and probably a dozen large wagons to transport provisions, etc. These require five yoke of oxen to each wagon. These, with the horses, men, etc., made up quite an imposing company.'

The dogs were, the paper assured its readers, 'the most magnificent pack of dogs there were ever seen in this country.' And Sir George Gore was 'a fine built, stout, light-haired and resolute looking man'.

When the train pulled out of Fort Laramie headed for North, Middle and Lost Parks in what is now Colorado, Joseph Chatillon, brother of Henry, was the chief guide.

The whole fantastic wagon train reached the Yapa River country of Wyoming and went into camp. Secretaries, mule skinners, guides, scouts, taxidermists and valet breathed a sigh of relief.

Sir William went his own way and Sir George began the first big shoot-out which was to net him two thousand buffalo, sixteen hundred deer and elk and over a hundred bears (including forty grizzlies) during the next two years.

He hunted deer with his pack of dogs. He hunted buffalo from a shooting stand and fired at the herds of the great lumbering beasts as scouts drove them into the valley.

Gun bearers handed Sir George loaded guns as fast as he could shoot. And afterwards Sir George strolled in the valley littered with the dead buffalo picking the few that his taxidermists would mount for exhibition in his trophy room in Brighton.

They went where no one but the mountain men and the Indians had been before and Joe Chatillon attested later that they went right through Middle Park, crossed the Continental Divide and 'camped on the four sides of Pike's Peak'.

Sir George had heard of the wonderful fishing to be had across the Continental Divide but there was no road across the mountains. Undeterred, he hired an entire tribe of one thousand Indians to rip a road out of the wilderness. Three weeks later, he was enjoying the word's finest fishing.

Four years later silver was discovered in the area and thousands of miners flocked into it. But at the time Sir George passed through it was virgin country.

Louis Dapron and two other scouts with the party discovered gold some seventy-five miles southwest of Fort Laramie in what is now Albany County, Wyoming, and being rough, uneducated men thought to show it to Sir George.

He laughed and told them it was mica and they threw it away.

Privately he told Chatillon: 'This is gold, but I did not come here to seek gold. I don't need it. This is a pleasure hunt.'

He struck camp at once and several years later when Dapron tried to re-locate his find he was unable to do so.

The party returned to Fort Laramie for the winter and there Sir George met one of the most colourful scouts and mountain men on the frontier. He was Jim Bridger, affectionately known as 'Ole Gabe', as renowned for his stories of wonders he had seen as he was for his skill as a trapper, Indian fighter and scout. Bridger had been the first white man to see the geysers in the Yellowstone basin and had mapped thousands of miles of wilderness. In the language of the mountain men 'Ole Gabe' had 'seen the elephant and heard the owl' in more strange places than most of his kind.

A. B. Ostrander, a young soldier who met Bridger a few years later, left a description of him which must have been much as he appeared to Sir George.

'His old battered hat had originally been of some light colour, but now looked like smoke,' the soldier wrote. 'His sack coat was of a dark grey material, and his brown corduroy breeches were reinforced on the seat and inside the thighs with buckskin, evidently to protect those parts while on horse-back.'

Sir George, fascinated by the gruff, almost monosyllabic frontiersman, employed him as chief scout. Bridger had probably never met an Englishman before, let alone an English baronet. He flatly refused to call Sir George by his title but out of respect always referred to his bluff employer as 'Mister Gore'.

Sir George was charmed by the illiterate Bridger and liked to yarn with him around the camp fires at evening.

They were an exotic pair. In clearings hundreds of miles from the nearest town or frontier fort the English baronet in his Norfolk jacket read Shakespeare's *As You Like It* to the rough frontiersman in his greasy buckskins.

And Bridger enjoyed it. Sir George's company brought out the best in him and Sir George found that after one hearing, Bridger's amazingly retentive mind could absorb great chunks of any play or book read out to him.

Captain Marcy, who got his material first-hand, reported this phase of Sir George's trip later and particularly mentioned the relationship between the English nobleman and Jim Bridger.

'His [Sir George's] favourite author was Shakespeare, which Bridger "reckon'd was a leetle too high-faulutin' for him"; moreover, he remarked that he "rather calculated that thar big Dutchman, Mr Full-stuff, was a leetle too fond of lager beer", and suggested that probably it might have been better for the old man if he had imbibed the same amount of alcohol in the more condensed medium of good old Bourbon whisky,' Marcy said.

'Bridger seemed deeply interested in the adventures of Baron Munchausen, but admitted, after the reading was finished, that "he be dogond ef he swallered everything that thar Baren Mountchawson said, and, he thout he was a durn'd liar". Yet, upon further reflection, he acknowledged that some of his own experiences among the Blackfeet would be equally marvellous, "ef writ down in a book".

'One evening Sir George entertained his auditor by reading to him Sir Walter Scott's account of the battle of Waterloo, and afterwards asked him if he did not regard that as the most sanguinary battle he had ever heard of. To which Bridger replied, "Wall, now Mr Gore, that thar must 'a bin a consideible of a skrimmage, dogon my skin ef it mustn't; them Britishers must 'a fit better thar than they did down to Horleans, whar Old Hickry gin um the forkedest sort 'o chain lightnin' that perhaps you ever did see in all yer born days!" And upon Sir George expressing a little incredulity in regard to the estimate Bridger placed upon the battle [of New Orleans], the latter added, "You can jist go yer pile on it, Mr Gore – you can, as sure as yer born".'

In the spring of 1855 they left Fort Laramie and headed for the North Platte. There they turned north to Caspar Creek and went up the Powder River to Dry Fork. It took them the whole year and as the new winter came on they went down Powder River to its confluence with the Yellowstone River then followed it to the mouth of the Tongue River which they went up for eight miles.

They built a fort to winter in, despite the fact that they were in the heart of hostile Indian country. In January, 1856, a band of Piegans, a branch of the Blackfoot tribe, made a raid on the horse herd and ran off twenty-one of the best animals. Sir

George's men tracked them for sixty miles but lost their tracks in a snowstorm.

To add to their troubles, Alexander Culbertson, the canny Scottish Agent for the American Fur Company, heard about Sir George's fort and that his men were trading with the friendly Crow Indians.

A month later Culbertson incited the Bloods, another branch of the Blackfoot tribe, to attack the horse herds. But Sir George's men beat them off and Big Plume, Culbertson's brother-in-law, was badly wounded.

Culbertson protested to Alfred J. Vaughan, Indian Agent for Upper Missouri, complaining about Sir George. Vaughan reported to his superiors that Gore's fort was one hundred feet square and that he was engaged in illegal trading with the Indians.

Soon afterwards Henry Bostwick accidentally set fire to a stand of timber near the fort and the pasture was burned out necessitating new grazing grounds for the horses. Sir George left some men at the fort and moved to a new pasture with his favourite horse, Steel Trap. They lived in a cabin Sir George had built and Steel Trap was fed on corn meal while less fortunate horses had to forage on cottonwood bark.

In April, 1856, the party headed for the Dakotas and once again one of the scouts discovered gold, this time on the headwaters of the Belle Fourche.

Jerry Proteau recalled the incident later: 'One Sunday I went to the falls of the Swift or Rapid Creek with Lamourie,' he said. 'As we were standing by the falls I noticed some yellow-looking stuff in the water, and I said to Lamourie – ' "By George, there's gold!" '

'I took off my shirt and scooped up three double handfuls of the yellow stuff, and put it in my shirt. Then Lamourie and I went back to camp. Sir George noticed me as we went back to camp, and asked me what I had in my shirt. I said, "Gold". He looked at it a little while, when (sic) he said, "O, no, Jerry, that's not gold; that's mica". I was not very well posted about gold and thought Sir George was. He took it and put it in two black bottles, and placed them in his chest. The next day we marched out of the Black Hills, and two or three days after Bridger told me that Sir George told him it *was* gold. Sir George also told Lamourie that if he would prospect on the head of Swift Creek he would find rich gold there.'

If he had admitted that it was gold, the great Indian Wars might have begun two decades earlier. For it was gold seekers in the sacred lands of the Sioux that sent the savage tribes on the warpath. Soon after this incident Jim Bridger left Sir George and his party to go about his own business.

The autumn of 1856–57 was spent in Fort Berthold and Sir George had troubles again. A man sold him some cattle at $50 a head and then upped his price by fifty per cent when Sir George needed more beef. The Englishman bought fifty head from the man's competitor and gave forty-four to the Hidasta Indians. It was an object lesson.

Sir George went to live with the Hidasta chief, Crow's Breast, in a tepee for a while and then moved back into the fort.

He travelled to Fort Union and met Vaughan who challenged his right to hunt in Indian tribal lands. Sir George produced a passport dated 24th May, 1854, issued in St Louis by Colonel Alfred Cumming, Superintendent of Indian Affairs for Central Division.

The six thousand mile hunt had cost the Eighth Baronet of Manor Gore nearly all the income from his Irish estates for three years and he decided to bring it to a close.

Sir George called on Alexander Culbertson at Fort Union and offered to sell him all the equipment of the expedition for less than a third of the cost.

Culbertson attempted to beat Sir George down by offering him only a tenth of the value. He was sure that he was on to a good thing as Sir George was anxious to return home.

But the canny Scots Agent bargained without Sir George's flaming temper and eccentric streak. The baronet stormed out of the room and left the fort. At his camp he gave orders for all the wagons to be hauled to the top of a high bluff where the river curved within sight of the fort.

He walked around the Indian encampment giving away beautifully engraved rifles worth hundreds of dollars and handing out stores and equipment enough to feed the entire Indian tribe for a year.

The rest of the equipment he carried up onto the bluff where the wagons had been drawn up in a cluster.

Then Sir George, carrying an enormous tarred stick, set fire to everything and stood back to admire his handiwork as the giant column of smoke from half a million dollars-worth of wagon train climbed slowly into the sky.

When the whole train was reduced to a vast pile of ashes, Sir George had the scrap-iron hurled from the cliff into the deep channel of the river so that Culbertson could not even salvage that.

Sir George's men built two flatboats to take the trophies to St Louis. He sent four men with them and then went overland himself with twelve men.

In 1875 he returned to America – but not to the West. He shot alligators and hunted birds in the swamps of Florida and then returned home.

On the last day of 1878 he died in Inverness, Scotland.

But today Colorado remembers him. The Gore Range of mountains and Gore Canyon are named after him. And nine thousand feet up in Colorado, at the top of Gore Pass, on State Highway 84, a few miles from the town of Kremmling, is a bronze plaque commemorating his crossing of the Continental Divide.

It was unveiled in 1956 by the State Historical Society of Colorado and reads:

GORE PASS

Altitude 9,000 feet

Here in 1855 crossed Sir George Gore an Irish Baronet bent on slaughter of game and guided by Jim Bridger. For three years he scoured Colorado, Montana and Wyoming, accompanied usually by forty men, many carts, wagons, hounds and unexampled camp luxuries. More than 2,000 buffalo, 1,600 elk and deer, 100 bears were massacred for sport.

CHAPTER EIGHT

THE SQUAW MAN

YOUNG William McGaa liked whisky and he liked women. His
father despaired of his ever becoming steady enough to settle
down and enter the church as the family had hoped he would.
They thought that sending him to America for a visit would help
to get the wildness out of him. But it did nothing of the kind.

For William McGaa liked what he saw West of the Mississippi. He grew to love the Indians and their wild, free life on
the plains. And he never returned to London. Instead he went
to what in the 1830s was the Far West – Montana, Wyoming
and Colorado. He ended up at Bent's Fort in Colorado and began the hazardous life of a trapper and Indian trader.

There he met John Simpson 'Blackfoot' Smith, a tough and
rugged young man who had been on the plains since 1826 and
knew them well. Smith had run away from his job as a tailor's
apprentice in St Louis and had ended up living with the Blackfeet Indians in Montana. But he had killed some of his hosts in
a private quarrel and fled to their traditional enemies the
Cheyennes. They called him Po-ome, which meant Blackfoot in
their tongue, and in time he settled down and married a
Cheyenne girl. He began to trade with the Indians and was at
Bent's Fort in 1838 when he met young William McGaa. Smith
had a reward of $500 on his head, put there by the Governor of
New Mexico, then still part of the republic of Mexico and
fanatically jealous of its rights. But nobody dared to try and claim
the reward, for 'Blackfoot' Smith – he was sometimes called 'Grey
Blanket' – was a hard man with either a gun or a knife.

He liked the young Englishman and took him under his wing.
They traded with the Cheyenne, Sioux and Arapahoe and after
one long, cold winter that McGaa spent in an Arapahoe encampment, he returned to Bent's Fort with an Arapahoe wife.

He worked with Smith right through the 1840s at Bent's Fort, along the Santa Fe Trail, at Fort Mann with mountain man Tom 'Broken Hand' Fitzpatrick, and occasionally, as he learned more of the ways of the plains, he made lone trading expeditions to the Utes and even the Comanches.

The decade came and went and with it the free, open life of the trader, mountain man and trapper. For settlers were beginning to push Westward in search of new homes and new lives on the frontier.

In late 1857 William McGaa and 'Blackfoot' Smith were camped along the South Platte River with their families and two Mexican traders. One morning they found a tiny nugget of gold in a stream and began to sift the gravel in the swift-running waters for more.

They moved their camp to what is now Cherry Creek, Colorado, and began working some abandoned Spanish diggings on the Platte River. They found a little silver, not a great deal, but some months afterwards a party of prospectors came into the area and found silver in quantities and also some gold.

The newcomers decided to lay out a town site and visited McGaa and Smith because, as they explained later, 'we thought they might help protect our interests to a certain extent, for the land belonged to the Arapahoe Indians'.

On 24th September, 1858, the town promoters – Adnah French, Charles Nichols, T. C. Dickson, John A. Churchill, William M. Smith, Frank M. Cobb and William Harley – admitted McGaa and Smith as the eighth and ninth members of the Committee who had decided to call the town St Charles. They drew up a constitution and by-laws, signed them and the following day Nichols, Cobb and Dickson surveyed three hundred and twenty acres of land into streets and house lots. It was agreed that McGaa, 'Blackfoot' Smith and Nichols should remain in possession of the land while the rest of the party went to Omaha, Nebraska, to buy supplies. The three men were to build a cabin on each quarter section of land in order to secure their claim to the townsite. McGaa received Certificate Number 1, dated 1st December, 1858, of the St Charles Town Association for Lot 1, Block 1, of the new settlement.

Several weeks later, while 'Blackfoot Smith and Nichols were away, another party arrived in the area. They had been sent by Governor Denver of Kansas to survey the soon-to-be-established Arapahoe County. They learned of the laying out of St Charles and of the silver strike and threatened William McGaa that if he did not cut them in on the deal they would see that the whole project was made void when the new county was established.

'They threatened that if I would not Interest said Commissioners appointed by Gov. Denver, they would eject me [,] tare (sic) down my cabins, give orders for me to leave the country, and threats also that Endanjered (sic) the Life of Myself and family,' McGaa reported later.

Having nobody to advise him McGaa eventually agreed to cut the newcomers in on the St Charles Company. They appointed Captain Bassett, William Parkinson, Theo Parkinson, Charles Rogers and 'Hickory' Rogers as top men and forced McGaa to expand the Company to forty. They also decided to rename the town Denver, in honour of the Kansas Governor, and drew up a new constitution and bye-laws. They surveyed two square miles of land and assigned McGaa seventy-two acres in an area called Cottonwood Point.

His cabin was built there and was the first cabin to be erected in Denver. His son William Denver McGaa was born there soon afterwards and achieved the distinction of being the first child born in what would later become the capital of the State of Colorado.

There was nothing that the original claimants of the St Charles Township could do about the newcomers' claims so they had to go along with them. The silver strike was on in earnest soon afterwards and 'Blackfoot' Smith and McGaa established a profitable ferry service across the Platte River to enable prospectors to get to a new boom township called Gregory.

Their homes, where once there had been open prairie, soon became hemmed in with other cabins along what became Ferry Street and McGaa lost some of his seventy-two acre holding to new arrivals during the initial rush to Denver.

For reasons known only to himself, McGaa had taken on a dual name somewhere along the line. He called himself, when it suited him, Jack Jones, and in time became almost as well-known under that name as he was under his real one.

Along with the miners and speculators came the writers and journalists to record their deeds. For Americans were very conscious at that time that they were creating history.

General William Larimer wrote later: 'Jack wanted everybody to know that he was more than an ordinary man. He commenced by telling me that his true name was William McGaa and that at one time his father had been Lord Mayor of London, which, of course, I had to believe whether true or not . . . [It was untrue.]

'Jack Jones and John Smith were almost inseparable, they built a cabin together, a sort of two-family affair. Smith had a son, John, who was about my age or perhaps a little younger: we often met on the hills hunting our ponies. The old man was very fond of him. John's mother was a Cheyenne. John was best contented when with the Indians and lost his life in the massacre at Sand Creek during the bloody onslaught of Col[onel] Chivington's command. Both Smith and Jones were very fond of horse racing and gambling. As the country became more thickly settled they drifted back to the farther frontier, civilized life and habits had no charm for them: they loved the Indians best.'

A pioneer journalist Frank Hall, who later became an historian, Territorial Secretary of Colorado and sometime Acting Governor, also met William McGaa. Years later he wrote of some of the squaw man's letters and credited him with fine penmanship and 'diction for the most part elegant and refined. After reading them it was difficult to reconcile the letters with the man himself, his appearance, habits and character,' Hall said. McGaa, for reasons known only to himself, told the journalist that he was Irish and had studied for the priesthood at Dublin.

William McGaa grew wealthy from his ferry and his land but he still occasionally pined for the old way of life and went with his wife to spend some time among her people. He fell in with a squawman named Robert North, a vicious renegade who would sell out his own people or the Arapahoes who had adopted him if the occasion demanded it.

In June, 1864, William McGaa and Robert North appeared before Governor John Evans of Colorado and made a deposition warning of an Indian uprising. They were not fully believed, but after Colonel John M. Chivington and the Colorado Volunteers massacred the peaceful camp of Chief Black Kettle and the Southern Cheyennes at Sand Creek in November, an Indian war started in earnest.

McGaa returned to Denver and in December gave half of his real estate properties to one Michael Jones in exchange for full clearance to the title of the Cottonwood Point Land – which had become F Street – a quarter section of land in West Denver and a three hundred and twenty acre holding known as the McGaa and Smith Ferry Landing.

He grew even wealthier and began to drink even more heavily. In December, 1866, he learned that Robert North had led the Arapahoe warriors in the attack on Captain William Fetterman near Fort Phil Kearny, Wyoming. Three years later North and his Arapahoe wife were captured by other renegades while on their way to a Southern Arapahoe camp and were hanged beside the trail.

As Denver became more and more civilised and akin to the best cities of the East and West coasts, men like McGaa and John Smith receded into the past. McGaa's drinking sprees became notorious and when the stage coach king Ben Holladay achieved fame and eminence in the city the name of McGaa Street was changed to honour the wealthy newcomer.

It was something which, said General Larimer, 'came nearer to breaking [McGaa's] heart than all the other vicissitudes of his life combined'.

Another child – this time a daughter, Jessie – was born to McGaa and his Arapahoe wife. The father continued to drink heavily.

On 14th December, 1867, he celebrated more vigorously than usual and was tossed into the jail to cool off. The next morning he was dead. William Byers's famed *Rocky Mountain News* carried an obituary on 16th December and was mercifully kind to the old man.

His father had always said that whisky would be the death of him.

CHAPTER NINE

THE ARTISAN

JAMES THORP was very proud of being an Englishman. The very fact that he was one saved his life.

He was born in Manchester in 1833 and in his early teens took a job in a textile mill. The wages were poor but he saved hard and by the time he was twenty he had put aside his fare to America. He went to Philadelphia in 1853 and there became a plasterer, stonemason and general builder. He enjoyed his new trade and working in stone gave him real pleasure. Three years after landing in America he emigrated to Missouri and settled near the little township of Miami which stands on a bluff and boasts one of the finest views of the Missouri River. There he married, built a three-roomed house and settled down.

Missouri was a slave-owning state and neighbouring Kansas was not. The storm clouds of the Civil War were gathering in 1856 when James Thorp arrived in Missouri and even though the actual Civil War did not break out until 1861 there was a virtual state of war between the slavers of Missouri and the abolitionists of Kansas.

The problem did not worry James Thorp over much and he prospered. He worked as a mason, built houses and carved tombstones and in 1860 his first child, a daughter, was born.

The War broke out the following year and men went off to fight but James Thorp did not go. Guerilla raiders rode in Kansas and Missouri but the Englishman was not troubled by them – for a time. The guerilla bands, most of them, nominally at least, riding for the Confederacy, were little more than organised brigades of pillagers, rapists and killers who frequently gave as little quarter to Southern sympathisers as to the Northerners. They were out for loot and did not care where it came from.

William Clarke Quantrell was feared throughout the mid-

Western states as the leader of the worst of the guerilla bands who burned, shot and pillaged their way across the land, but some of his lieutenants were little better than he.

Two of them were George Todd and 'Bloody Bill' Anderson who both were to come into contact with the young stonemason from Manchester. So were a party of his men, some of whom were later to become household names in the West. For riding with Todd and Anderson were Jesse and Frank James, Arch Clement and the Younger brothers, all of them destined to become outlaws at the end of the Civil War.

George Todd, brutal and dangerous, was, so a contemporary said, 'a man of iron who would have a go at a circular saw'.

'Bloody Bill' Anderson had had a sister killed when a building collapsed and he believed that Union troops had undermined it. He carried a silk cord in which he tied a knot for every Yankee he killed to avenge her death.

Arch Clement, from Kingville, Johnson County, Missouri, though only twenty years old in 1864, was a shrewd and calculating killer who Frank James, looking back in later years, described as 'the real brains of Anderson's outfit'.

In September, 1864, Todd and Anderson, who usually operated separate guerilla bands, joined forces to ride to Jefferson City, Missouri, to meet Confederate General Sterling Price and attack the city. Anderson planned to stop by the town of Fayette on the way and burn it out in retaliation for the deaths of six of his men who had been killed by its citizens some weeks before. They stopped there but unexpectedly found a Federal garrison stationed in the town and were beaten off with the loss of another six men.

Riding north the guerilla band were in a meaner than usual mood. Word of their coming spread ahead of them and all citizens in their path hid their valuables and took to the hills where possible.

The story of their arrival at the town of Miami and of their meeting with James Thorp is told by Raymond W. Thorp, his son. It is a tale the family have handed down.

'The road which led down the river bluffs on which Miami was located was known as the Brunswick Road. This road came through Miami and passed my father's house at the east end of town. However, a jutting bank shut off view of my father's house from the main road; the house could only be seen if one entered a lane which ran past it to the river. Now, on this quiet, serene Sunday – never a day of work for James Thorp – my father, his wife and his little child sat in the shade of pear trees which he had planted, and looked down the mighty river. Trouble and the war seemed far away.

'Down from Jackson County, travelling the Brunswick Road, came the most savage, ruthless, and deadliest crew of men who ever sat on the backs of horses. They came like a swarm of locusts, consuming everything along the way, and when they had passed, countless men, and even women and children, swung from trees along the way. They left Lexington a shambles. They were three hundred and fifty in number, riding in a column of fours, and at their head rode 'Bloody Bill' Anderson. Along the way they confiscated horses, food, guns and ammunition; every house was searched, and according to the humour of Anderson, the occupants either killed or lectured. These were the men who had sacked, pillaged, and burned Lawrence, Kansas, twice. They had burned men alive along the Santa Fe Trail, and many of them carried scalps on the headstalls of their bridles.

'The people of Miami had been apprised, and all were in their cyclone cellars, as word had been sent ahead that if no opposition was met, they would spare Miami's houses and Miami's citizens if they were allowed to pillage in peace.

'James Thorp, living away at the eastern edge of town, had not been apprised; there had not been time; the people went underground like rabbits. But seated in his yard, on that quiet day, he suddenly heard the ominous sound that only the hooves of hundreds of horses could make. Now and then he heard a yell, and shots. He looked towards the road, but the cutbank shut off his view.

'He said to his wife: "Take the child into the cellar," for he had an inkling of the situation.

'As he stood in his yard the great cavalcade was sweeping past on the Brunswick Road. He hoped they would pass him up because of the cutbank, but such was not his luck. A dozen guerillas rode into the lane; looked up and saw the house on the bluff.

'Bill Anderson was at their head; he gave an order to one of his men, and the fellow rode down and stopped the cavalcade at the red bridge which spanned the creek. Here the main band dismounted, spread up and down the creek, watered their horses, and sat in the shade. Besides the horses they rode, there were five hundred head of the finest animals in Missouri that they had picked up along the way.

'Now, Bill Anderson and his picked crew rode up the hill, and into my father's yard.

'The huge, blackbearded killer, who carried eight revolvers and a hatchet in his belt, and two dragoon pistols in saddle holsters, said: "Well, man, have you got any guns we can use? We're headed for Centralia, and we're going to kill every blue-belly we see. We haven't got enough guns to do it all."

'My father looked at the arsenal of each man and wondered why.

'He said: "I never use guns."

'Two men went in and ransacked the house, and came out again.

'One said: "Captain, he don't seem to have any guns."

'The guerilla chief looked at him and said: "Did you boys look under the bed?"

'The bushwhackers went back into the house, and shortly reappeared, carrying a Yager rifle, two shotguns, and four Colt's revolvers. Anderson picked up an end of his heavy beard and chewed on it. It was well known throughout Missouri that when Bill Anderson chewed his beard, death was not far away.

'He said to James Thorp: "Why did you lie, man?"

'My father hadn't lied, but he knew there was no use in explanations.

'The two men who had ransacked the house led my father over to a young walnut tree with a horizontal limb, placed a noose about his neck, threw it over the limb and drew it taut.

'One of Bill Anderson's favourite lieutenants was a smooth-faced lad – a boy named Arch Clement. He was not over twenty years of age, and had killed more than three hundred men. He had burned men at the stake, and from his bridle new scalps fluttered in the breeze.

'My father knew Arch and his entire family, and now said to

him: "Arch, you know me, and that I never use a gun. The guns were given to me for work, by people who had no cash."

'Arch Clement did not care to beard "Bloody Bill", who had a revolver in his hand, ready to fire the signal for the rope to be pulled.

'He replied: "This is your trouble, man, not mine," and rode to the edge of the yard and looked away down the river.

'Bill Anderson said: "Man, speak up before I fire this pistol. Give me one good reason why I shouldn't fire it, and you go free."

'James Thorp knew he was doomed despite anything he might say. But he had nothing to lose now, and everything to gain. He managed a foolish remark.

'He said: "I have nothing to do with this war. But I warn you – if you hang me you will have to answer to the Queen!"

'Time stood still then. What Queen? What nonsense! Speaking of a monarch thousands of miles across the sea to a man who had never heard of a Queen? A man who, if he had had Abe Lincoln on that tree, would have cut pieces from his body at intervals between gloating? A man who feared neither God nor Devil? A man who had been known to cut off the upreaching arms of beseeching victims?

'Arch Clement had heard. He swivelled his horse and rode over to them.

'Bill Anderson said: "Arch, you know this man. What in the hell does he mean?"

'Arch, who had left school during his first week for a career of blood, and who could neither read nor write, nevertheless saw his chance to save one whom he knew to be innocent, who had appealed to him and had been denied.

'He said: "He's right, Bill. He don't belong here. He's an Englishman."

'For many minutes after the guerillas had gone James Thorp sat still in his yard, too weak to rise. He thanked God, and Queen Victoria, and men who feared only one thing, the unknown. His guns still lay in the yard; he gathered them up and carried them into the house. Then he went and lifted the cellar door, and told his wife to come out.

'The three stood in the yard and looked down towards the red

bridge over the creek, watched guerillas as they tightened their
saddle cinches, gathered up their extra horses and baggage, and
rode away down the Brunswick Road, toward Centralia. Then
my father went down to the creek and cut down the swinging
bodies of two unfortunate Negroes who had furnished sport for
the knife-throwing bushwhackers as they kicked in their death
throes. The black men hadn't known the key word to survival
"Queen".

'This is the story that has come down in the Thorp family. It
has never varied in the telling!'

Three days later – on the 27th September – the guerillas entered Colombia, held up a stage but found nobody readily
identifiable as a Federal sympathiser and allowed it to go on.

Soon afterward they reached Centralia and the westbound
passenger train pulled into the station.

A party of sixty-one guerillas, including 'Bloody Bill', George
Todd, Jesse and Frank James, Jim Younger, Captain Harrison
Trow and Captain Johnny Thrailkill found seventy-five Federal
soldiers on the train. They were going home on leave. One was
kept to be exchanged for a captured guerilla. The others were
shot out of hand and the train was set on fire and sent flying
off down the tracks.

W. F. Bassett, of the U.S. Military Telegraph, who arrived
soon after the massacre, told the St Joseph *Argus* about it several
days later.

'About 11 o'clock the rumbling of the railway train could be
heard as it thundered down the grade and slowed at the depot,
its occupants being entirely oblivious that they were on the
threshold of a monstrous tragedy,' Bassett said. 'Scarcely had
the train ground to a halt, however, before the soldiers aboard –
75 in number – glanced out of the windows and at once com-
prehended the situation.'

After the killing was over, Bassett added, 'A full head of steam
was turned on and the engine sent flying tenantless away to the
North.' The townspeople got busy 'digging a long ditch near
where the soldiers were killed, [and] buried them in one common grave'.

The guerillas rode away and the same day, ten miles from
Centralia, near Paris, seat of Monroe County, gave battle to a

battalion of raw State Militia commanded by Major A. E. V. Johnson who had ridden from the town boasting that he would return 'with the head of Anderson on a pole'.

George Todd ordered seventeen-year-old Jesse James to accompany Ole Shepherd and Peyton Long and act as decoys. Then the guerillas charged. Only five of Johnson's troops – they numbered nearly two hundred – escaped alive.

Reported Bassett: 'Rapidly a puff of smoke would be seen, and then another horse would be riderless and dash off into the gathering twilight. But five of the whole command escaped slaughter. Jesse James was accredited with nine victims on the case; Ole Shepherd eight; George Todd eight; Peyton Long seven; Blake Hudspeth six and the others from three to five each. The guerillas lost but one, a young beardless boy who had joined them the day before in Howard County.'

Jesse James, then a few days past his seventeenth birthday, killed nine men that day. One of them was Major Johnson. He stripped the body of its equipment and gave the dead man's belt and pistol to Ole Shepherd's brother George. He gave the pistol he killed Johnson with to his own brother, Frank James.

The men who were present when James Thorp had the inspiration to let Queen Victoria save his life all had violent lives – and most of them violent deaths.

'Bloody Bill' Anderson was killed on 27th October, 1864, near Missouri City. The silk cord he carried to tally Federal soldiers he killed had fifty-four knots in it. His head was cut off and put on a telegraph pole.

George Todd was killed in a battle at Waverly, near Lexington, Missouri, on 23rd October, 1864, just four days before Anderson's death.

Arch Clement was with Jesse James at Lexington on 23rd April, 1865, when they tried to surrender. A soldier shot Jesse in the chest but they escaped. Clement nursed him back to health and rode with him into Liberty, Missouri, on 13th February, 1866, when twelve ex-guerillas held up Clay County Savings Association. Later he was killed at Lexington.

Jesse James became America's most famous outlaw and after sixteen years of banditry was killed in St Joseph, Missouri, on 3rd April, 1882.

Frank James rode with his brother as an outlaw, surrendered after Jesse's death and lived until 18th February, 1918.

James Thorp, the quick-witted Englishman, lived on to raise eight children by his first wife and another brood by his second wife.

CHAPTER TEN

THE INDIAN FIGHTER

RED CLOUD, the mighty Sioux chief, rose slowly to address the Peace Commissioners. His words were carefully weighed and measured and the interpreter cast apprehensive glances at the seated soldiers and civilians as he began to translate the chieftain's gutteral speech.

'My people came to this place to talk peace, but the White Eagle is not here for peace; you cannot talk peace with so many soldiers,' Red Cloud began.

'I say he is here to steal the country of our fathers, and to build an iron trail for the fireboat which walks on mountains and frightens away our game. If this is so, there is no reason for more empty words; if it is so, my people will fight.'

Red Cloud paused.

Colonel Henry B. Carrington, the man the chief had called White Eagle because of the silver eagle which was his insignia of rank, stirred uneasily. He was not there to build a railroad as Red Cloud believed. But the chief was right in thinking that the soldiers were not there for peace. For Carrington's orders were to build a chain of three military forts to protect travellers along the Bozeman trail to the Montana goldfields.

Red Cloud spoke again.

'I'll kill every white man who goes beyond Crazy Woman's Fork of the Powder River,' he warned.

Then, pulling his blanket tighter round his lean, hard body, he turned on his heel and strode from the Fort Laramie peace council without a backward glance. One by one his men followed him.

The peace conference broke up. His job, Carrington knew, would not be an easy one.

He led his long column of the Eighteenth United States Infantry out of Fort Laramie and started north. Old Fort Connor was rebuilt, re-named Fort Reno, garrisoned and the column moved on. On 14th July, 1866, they began to build a new fort right in the heart of the Sioux hunting ground.

It was called Fort Phil Kearny.

Red Cloud's warriors watched from the hills, waited for the chance and struck suddenly and savagely. On nine occasions during the first fifteen days they attacked small parties of soldiers cutting wood for the fort. In August they captured two soldiers and tortured them to death over a slow fire. In September they ran off the beef herd. But Carrington's men worked on. They cut down trees with their rifles stacked close by. They hauled tree trunks to the fort site while outriders patrolled the trail ahead with guns ready. And on 31st October, 1866, the log stockade was finished and the first garrison flag was raised over Fort Phil Kearny.

They were secure for the winter for the Sioux dared not attack the fort. But raids on the wood trains and on small parties of troops continued.

On 6th December an officer and a sergeant were killed within sight of the fort. Then, four days before Christmas, eighty-one men under the command of cocky young Captain William Fetterman, who completely under-estimated the fighting abilities of the Sioux, rode out to protect a wagon train hauling wood and were wiped out to a man. The fort, desperately under-manned now, prepared for an all out attack by the Indians. The women and children were placed in the underground powder magazine, ready to be blown up if the Sioux overwhelmed the fort.

A scout named John 'Portugee' Phillips – he was born in the Azores – volunteered to make the near-suicidal ride of two hundred and thirty-six miles to Fort Laramie to bring help. He rode out on Colonel Carrington's prize Kentucky thoroughbred and reached Fort Laramie on Christmas Eve.

Early in the new year a relief column fought their way through snow drifts to reach Fort Phil Kearny. Colonel Carrington was relieved of his command and sent back East in disgrace because of the Fetterman affair. The cocky officer had disobeyed his Colonel's orders and had been lured into a trap which led to the deaths of his entire command. But jealous officers submitted private reports to the Department Headquarters and Carrington was blamed. It took him thirty years to clear his name.

Private Samuel Gibson, an eighteen-year-old Englishman serving in C Company, Twenty-First United States Infantry, was at Fort Phil Kearny throughout the Red Cloud War.

'Colonel Carrington was blamed by the Government, and a criticising public, for this disaster, whereas Fetterman alone was to blame for it,' Gibson said later. 'I happened to be on guard at the west gate of the fort on that fatal morning, when Fetterman and his men passed out the gate, and I distinctly heard Colonel Carrington order Fetterman to follow the wood train and not leave it under any circumstances whatever.'

Samuel Gibson was born in England in 1849 and moved to the United States with his family in 1865. The following year he enlisted in the United States Army at Cleveland, Ohio, and was assigned to the Eighteenth Infantry, then stationed at Fort Kearney, Nebraska. He had marched into Montana with Carrington and had helped in the building of Fort Phil Kearny.

In June, 1867, a civilian wagon train creaked into the fort bringing with it a supply of new, rapid-loading rifles to replace the outmoded single-shots the troops had been issued with. The men were keen to try them out.

They did not have long to wait.

On the edge of a flat plain about six miles from Phil Kearny civilian contractors maintained a base camp for men employed to cut wood for the fort. A detachment of troops was always stationed with them to protect the loggers from marauding Indian bands.

On the last day of July Private Samuel Gibson and C Company rode out of the fort to begin a month-long tour of guard duty. They pitched their tents outside a small corral constructed from the bodies of wagons which had been detached from their wheels and set in a circle to provide shelter for the loggers.

The Sioux struck two days later.

Early in the morning of 2nd August mounted Indians appeared on the skyline and small parties swept down the slopes and attacked groups of soldiers and civilians who were cutting wood. One party of men which included 'Portugee' Phillips, raced for the fort while the others fought their way back to the corral of wagon boxes and waited for a full-scale attack.

Private Samuel Gibson was running for his life and a band of mounted Sioux were gaining on him as he neared the corral. Then Sergeant Max Littman, a tough German-born soldier, ran from the wagon-box corral and opened fire on the Indians. They swerved away from the running man and Gibson reached the corral safely with Littman at his heels.

He flung himself into a wagon-box occupied by two Irish soldiers, Sergeant McQuiery and Private John Grady. Both were experienced Indian fighters. Gibson was not. He had never been under fire.

'When I took my place in the wagon-box both of them had their shoes off, and were fixing their shoestrings into loops to fit over the right foot and from thence to the trigger of their rifles – to kill themselves when all hope was lost,' Private Gibson recalled years later. 'If the Indians passed over our barricades by an over-whelming force of numbers, every man would stand erect, place the muzzle of his loaded rifle under his chin and take his own life rather than be captured and made to endure the inevitable torture.'

Gibson had just made loops from his own shoelaces when the Sioux charged. Inside the little wagon-box corral were thirty-two soldiers and civilians preparing to sell their lives dearly. Red Cloud personally commanded nearly three thousand warriors, the fighting might of the Sioux nation.

'Resting my rifle on the top of the wagon-box I began firing with the rest,' Gibson remembered. 'The whole plain was alive with Indians, all mounted and visible in every direction. They were riding madly about, and shooting at us with guns, bows and arrows, first on one side and then on the other of the corral.

'Then they would circle, and each time come in closer, utter-ing the most piercing and unearthly war cries. The tops of the wagon beds were literally ripped and torn to slivers with their bullets.'

The new rifles blazed out a solid wall of death at the advancing Indians and they withdrew, puzzled and frightened by the speed with which the white men were able to reload their guns and fire again.

Recalled Gibson: 'The plain in front of us was strewn with dead and dying Indians and ponies. The Indians were amazed, but not by any means daunted. They were there for blood, and came in such hordes that they were ready for any sacrifice if they could but capture our little party.'

The Indians gathered and regrouped and then charged again. Suddenly Private John Grady realised that the troop's tents would restrict the field of fire if the Sioux managed to get really close. He leapt from the wagon-box and sprinted out to pull down the tents.

'I followed him, with the bullets zipping about us and the arrows swishing past and striking the ground on all sides of us,' Gibson recalled. 'We loosened the loops around the tent-pins at the corners, working together until all but the last of the tents had dropped. Amid a perfect hail of bullets and arrows we rushed back and leapt over into our wagon beds again.'

Lieutenant John C. Jenness went down as the Indians swept round the wagon-box corral; Private Henry Haggerty, a tough little man from Jersey in the Channel Islands, was killed; Private Tommy Doyle suddenly stood erect and then toppled over with a bullet between the eyes.

The Sioux raced by once more and then retreated.

The fight had been going on for more than four hours and the midday sun was overhead. The men began calling from wagon-box to wagon-box asking for water. The only water barrel had been riddled with bullets and its precious contents had run away. Few of the men had full canteens but those who had shared them with their comrades. Outside the corral, midway between the wagon-boxes and the tents, were two camp kettles which had somehow escaped being hit. Privates Gibson and Grady slipped from their protecting cover and crawled out to bring the kettles back. The Sioux saw the move and opened fire. Gibson's kettle was hit twice and some of the water was lost but they got back safely.

'It must have been three o'clock in the afternoon when we distinctly heard a sort of humming sound, seemingly made by many voices, below us in the Big Piney Valley,' Gibson said. 'Some of us thought it was the squaws wailing over their dead warriors. As we waited in silent wonderment at this strange sound, unlike anything we had ever heard before, it appeared to come from the northwest of the corral. The Indians to the east and south of us had come out on to the plain, where they were circling and coming nearer all the time, brandishing their spears and war clubs at us and giving voice to their war cries.

'Those of the warriors who were armed with guns immediately opened fire upon us, and we at once replied, killing and wounding many more of them. During this time, that awful humming and chanting sound grew in volume and intensity, coming nearer and nearer, now directly from the west of us. The Indians to the south had withdrawn out of range, and seemed to be waiting for something to happen.'

The waiting was over soon enough.

For, suddenly, streaming out of a ravine came a V-shaped wedge of near-naked warriors. They were all on foot and Red Cloud's nephew, a magnificent Indian in a gigantic war bonnet, was in the lead.

'Immediately we opened a terrific fire on them, under which nothing could stand and at the very first volley Red Cloud's nephew fell, pierced by many bullets,' Gibson recalled. 'They were so close that it seemed as if nothing could prevent their swarming over our barricade and into the corral, when it would have been all over with us in no time. Then, just when it seemed as if all hope was gone, the Indians suddenly broke and fled. They could not stand up before the withering fire we poured into their ranks.'

About four o'clock in the afternoon the tired troops heard the booming of a mountain field gun as a column of soldiers from Fort Phil Kearny fought their way on to the plain to bring relief.

'We all jumped to our feet and yelled,' said Gibson. 'We threw our caps in the air. We hugged each other in the ecstasy of our joy. We laughed, cried and fairly sobbed like little children in the delirium of our delight. The awful strain was over.'

The Sioux withdrew taking with them as many of their dead and wounded as they could carry. The majority of the dead warriors were left where they fell. Red Cloud said later that the thirty-two men in the wagon-boxes had killed or wounded eleven hundred of his finest warriors.

Fort Phil Kearny and Fort C. F. Smith, another fort Carrington had built, were abandoned exactly a year later. On 2nd August, 1868, United States troops rode away from the lonely fort on the Big Piney. Red Cloud had made good his threat and the U.S. Government had given in.

It was the only Indian war they ever lost.

Private Samuel Gibson saw service with the Army in the Sioux campaigns of 1876 – during which Custer was killed on the Little Big Horn and Crook was defeated on the Rosebud – and was a sergeant in H Company, Twenty-Second Infantry during the Ghost Dance War, the last clash between the Sioux and U.S. troops in 1890–91.

In all, he completed forty-eight years in the Army.

'But never, before or since, have my nerves been put to the test they sustained on that terrible 2nd August, 1867, when we fought Red Cloud's warriors at the wagon-box corral,' he said shortly before he died.

CHAPTER ELEVEN

THE VIGILANTE

THE two men stood silently on the small stools. There could be no escape. Their hands were tied behind their backs and there were nooses around their necks. Above the whining of the January wind a voice with a cultured English accent rang out.

'Men, do your duty.'

The stool was jerked from beneath G. W. Brown and he died without a sound. Erastus 'Red' Yager followed him to hell a few seconds later.

The vigilantes mounted up and rode away. The two bodies were left beside the trail through Stinkingwater Valley, Montana Territory. Pinned to the back of Yager was a notice which said: RED! ROAD AGENT AND MESSENGER. On the other body a notice said: BROWN! CORRESPONDING SECRETARY.

It was 4th January, 1864.

As silently as they had come the twenty-four vigilantes left. Back in Virginia City, Montana Territory, they re-assembled at their headquarters, a general store.

Thomas James Dimsdale, the Englishman with the party, presented a sheaf of notes to the others. They were headed in a delicate copper-plate: 'Confession of Erastus 'Red' Yager, Member of The Innocents'. Dimsdale's notes represented the final and vital link in a long campaign by the Virginia City Vigilantes to smash The Innocents, the most daring, best organised and ruthless of the gangs which terrorised the mining camps of Montana.

That night, back in his two-roomed clap-board house Thomas Dimsdale faced again the fact that he probably did not have long to live. He vowed once more that he would see The Innocents smashed before his time came.

He had been born in England in 1831 and had been well

educated. He was a Professor of English at Oxford University in
1861 when doctors diagnosed his hacking cough as tuberculosis.
They recommended that high, mountain air might prolong his
life a little.

He tried Canada at first but did not like it. Then he heard of
the gold strikes in Montana Territory, across the border in the
United States. Gold had been found near Virginia City and men
from many parts of the world had flocked there to search for it
– a ruthless few prepared to kill for it.

He arrived in the summer of 1863 but soon found that he was
physically too weak to handle the heavy sluice boxes that miners
trapped the gold dust in. He looked around for some other way
to make a living and opened a small private school – tuition $2
a week – and gave singing lessons in the evenings. Dimsdale drew
to himself all that was best in Virginia City. His friend Granville
Stuart described him as 'a gentle, kind-hearted Christian man'.

The crime rate in Montana was soaring. Men were robbed in
broad daylight; murders were every-day occurrences; mule trains
laden with ore were plundered on lonely trails; killers openly
walked the streets, pushing innocent bystanders off the sidewalks
and insulting respectable women. The law did nothing.

A smooth-talking Bostonian, Henry Plummer, was the Sheriff
and he took no action in any of the crimes. His deputies were
tough, badge-wearing killers who idled around the saloons. Dimsdale's indignation at Plummer's idleness turned to suspicion when
he noticed a curious coincidence. Many of the men in the district
who appeared to have plenty of money without working, wore
goatee beards and tied their ties in a sailor's knot.

Late December, 1863, the outlaws overplayed their hand when
they killed a popular young German named Nick Tbalt. He was
found dead and frozen stiff in some bushes just off a main trail.
He had been badly beaten and then dragged at a rope's end over
rough ground. Evidence pointed to one of Sheriff Plummer's
friends, George Ives, and he was arrested. An impromptu miners'
court tried and convicted him of murder and he was hanged.

After Ives's execution the Montana Vigilantes were born. They
met in a store in Virginia City and planned their next moves in
the drive to rid Montana of killers. A German, John X. Beidler
was elected hangman.

'Red' Yager and G. W. Brown were the first to be captured by the Vigilantes.

When they told the outlaws that they would be hanged Brown begged for mercy but Yager just shrugged.

'It is pretty rough but I merited this years ago,' he said. 'I know all about the gang and there are men in it who deserve this more than I do; but I should die happy if I could see them hanged, or know that it would be done. I don't say this to get off; I don't want to get off.'

He told them to bring a pencil and write down his confession. Dimsdale noted down everything the condemned man said. And that night the Vigilantes studied the confession; it named names and it gave details of the organisation of the biggest of the outlaw gangs – The Innocents.

Yager said that Sheriff Henry Plummer was the leader of the gang and that his deputies were the chief lieutenants. They had killed one hundred and two men in a little over a year. And he provided a list of roadagents and other Innocents.

The Vigilantes planned carefully and then went into action. On 10th January they captured Sheriff Henry Plummer and his deputies Buck Stinson and Ned Ray in Bannack.

They dragged Plummer to the scaffold that he had had built for a legal hanging and he broke down. Playing for time, and hoping for a deliverance by his friends, he asked to see his sister-in-law, demanded trial by jury, called on God to damn the Vigilantes, and offered to leave the country forever.

'Can't you see, boys, that I'm too wicked to die?' he asked.

Pitilessly the Vigilantes' hangman, X. Beidler executed deputies Stinson and Ray.

By the time Plummer's turn came he had recovered his nerve.

'Give a man time to pray,' he said.

'Certainly,' Thomas Dimsdale called back. 'But do it up there.' And he pointed to the gallows.

Beidler put the rope around the outlaw sheriff's neck.

'You are hanging an Innocent man,' Plummer joked grimly. And then: 'Give me a good drop, boys.'

They did.

Two other Innocents were hanged in Bannack the following day and the Vigilantes captured five more of the gang in Virginia

City on 14th January. They were hanged in a half-built store. Boone Helm, one of the men, had an unsavoury reputation for cannibalism which stretched from Oregon to Canada and back. Another Innocent trod air two days afterwards and five days later they hanged Bill Bunton, named by 'Red' Yager as Plummer's second-in-command. Another man was hanged at Frenchtown on 24th January and the following day the Vigilantes executed four more Innocents at the appropriately-named Hell's Gate. On 26th January they hanged a man at Fort Owens and the last man died in the Gallatin Valley on 3rd February.

A horde of lesser lights named by Yager were banished along with two lawyers who had defended George Ives in court. The Innocents were broken and other criminal gangs moved away from Montana where the threat of stretched necks was all too great.

Montana became a State on 26th May, 1864. Governor Edgerton appointed Thomas Dimsdale to the post of superintendent of public schools and he served in this capacity for nearly two years. That summer the Vigilantes rode again and a number of outlaws who had drifted back to Montana learned to their cost that the hard-riding executioners were still active.

Thomas Dimsdale turned to journalism and became the first editor of the *Montana Post*. His press and equipment travelled from St Louis, Missouri, to Fort Benton, Montana, by riverboat and were then taken overland to Virginia City. On 26th August, 1865, he published the first of a long series of articles telling about the Montana Vigilantes and their war with The Innocents. Early the following year he issued it as a book – the first to be published in Montana – under the title of *The Vigilantes of Montana*.

But Dimsdale's health was failing. The long rides in the first few months of 1864 had taken a lot out of him. He died at the age of thirty-five on 22nd September, 1866.

CHAPTER TWELVE

THE LADY GAMBLER

THE old saying 'lucky at cards, unlucky at love' held good for 'Poker Alice', a young Suffolk girl who became the acknowledged Queen of the Western gamblers, smoked black cigars and packed a six-shooter she was not scared to use.

Alice Ivers was born in Sudbury, Suffolk, on 17th February, 1851, the daughter of a local schoolteacher. Gently reared, she grew into an intelligent and likeable blonde girl and was twelve years old when her family decided to emigrate to America.

Richmond, Virginia, in 1863 was a far cry from a little country village. The clouds of the Civil War raged over the Confederate capital that year – a crucial one for the South. But the new arrivals settled in and Alice's father had little trouble finding a job as a teacher. Most of the local schoolmasters were away at the front and the schools were crying out for masters. Two years later the Confederacy surrendered and crumbled and the boys in blue and grey came marching home. Alice Ivers and her family left war-torn Richmond and moved West to Colorado.

Denver, the capital, was a different picture again. On the edge of a raw frontier, the town was built around the fabulous silver mines which had lured adventurers to the West in 1858. Most of the houses were log cabins, a few were brick built.

The Suffolk teacher got a good job in a local school and it was through him that Alice met mining engineer Frank Duffield.

'It was love at first sight,' Alice recalled many years later.

Alice was only 19. Duffield was 27. But her parents approved of the match and the young couple were married in 1870 and moved to Lake City, Colorado, where Duffield was employed as an engineer.

But tragedy was only round the corner.

Alice and Frank had been married less than a year when he was killed in a mine cave-in.

Destitute, Alice looked round for a way to support herself. She could have taught in a school, but Lake City at the time did not have one. Most women would have borrowed the money and returned home, but Alice was made of sterner stuff. She had watched her husband playing cards, and in the long evenings when he was in the saloons in poker games she had entertained herself playing patience. She was a natural calculator and her long slim fingers manipulated the cards deftly.

One night, soon after Frank Duffield's death, she asked a saloon owner to let her play a few hands with the regulars. He was sufficiently impressed to hire Alice to deal cards for a percentage of the winnings. And Alice Duffield was in business and earning her nickname, 'Poker Alice'. She did well in Lake City. But she had an urge to travel, and left for Silver City, New Mexico, where new mines were producing.

She arrived with only ten dollars in her pocket and went into the first saloon she saw. She sat in on a faro game and won. She bet again. Neither 'Poker Alice' nor the dealer realised that she was embarking on one of the most fabulous gambling 'dutchies' in the history of New Mexico. Every time she bet, she won, and soon other players had dropped out leaving only 'Poker Alice' and the dealer. Eventually he lost his nerve and declared the bank closed.

'Then move over,' snapped 'Poker Alice' contemptuously, 'and give someone who wants to gamble, a chance.'

She opened her bank with the winnings and by the time she was ready to go, over $100,000 had passed across the table and she had a clear profit of $10,000.

From Silver City she went back to Colorado. In Leadville she lost all her money. In Central City she won it all back again. Once more in New Mexico, this time in Georgetown, she added to her bank balance and left for Texas.

Women gamblers were a rarity in those days on the frontier and 'Poker Alice' was one of the first. She took to carrying a gun and smoking long black cigars.

A dealer in a Pecos, Texas, saloon thought that he had an easy customer in the little blonde woman with the English accent.

'Poker Alice' soon caught him dealing cards off the bottom of the deck. For a few hands she watched him closely. The dealer, unaware that he was being observed, carried on cheating. Suddently 'Poker Alice' pushed back her chair, raked in the 'pot' with her left hand and pulled her gun with her right.

'If you'd cheated cleverly I wouldn't have minded, but you're too clumsy,' she told him tartly. 'I never could stand a clumsy crook.'

'Poker Alice' had collected about $5,000, so she packed her six-shooter in a carpetbag and set out for New York. She went on a week-long spending spree buying clothes and jewellery and dining in exclusive restaurants and then returned to the West – broke but happy. It became the pattern of her life. A big win in the West followed by a big spree in the East. Easy come, easy go.

The little woman with the neat blonde hair, blue eyes and deadpan expression became a familiar figure in every boom town from St Louis to San Francisco and from Canada to the Mexican border. Often she was extravagantly dressed, but she always wore her Colt revolver, and always had a long black cheroot stuck in the side of her mouth.

She had her own code too: 'I have never run a crooked game and never gamble on a Sunday,' she liked to say.

In 1892 there was a silver 'rush' to Creede in Colorado and 'Poker Alice' was among the early arrivals.

She got a job in the Number 10 Saloon which was owned by a man renowned in American folklore and song as 'the dirty little coward who shot Mr Howard'. He was Bob Ford, the man who had shot America's most famous outlaw, Jesse James, in the back for the sake of the reward money. At the time of the killing James was living under the alias of Thomas Howard.

Hated, feared and despised, Bob Ford had reached the end of the line. He was twice run out of Creede by irate miners and then allowed back on the promise of good behaviour.

But on 9th June, 1892, an enemy named Edward O. Kelley tracked him down and killed him with a double-barrelled shotgun mostly because he wanted to be known as 'the man who killed the man who killed Jesse James'.

'Poker Alice' was sitting in at a gaming table when Ford was killed. His death meant the end of her job, and, disliking Creede, she moved on.

In early 1893 she was in Deadwood, South Dakota, working in a saloon. The other 'house gambler' was William G. Tubbs and a friendly rivalry developed between them.

Some two months after arriving in Deadwood 'Poker Alice' was dealing cards at her table when a drunken miner accused the unarmed Tubbs of cheating and attacked him with a Bowie knife. As the miner lunged, a shot rang out. He dropped the knife and grabbed his arm cursing. 'Poker Alice' stood by her table, a wisp of smoke curling from the barrel of her sixgun.

'Poker Alice' and Tubbs, gambling rivals, were married soon afterwards and retired from the gaming tables. They bought a farm some forty-eight miles from Sturgis, South Dakota, adopted seven orphan children and raised chickens. But that life was not to last.

During a blizzard in 1910 Tubbs died of pneumonia. 'Poker Alice' dragged his body into a backroom cut off from the house and the corpse soon froze. As soon as the wind dropped a little she put the body on a sleigh and dragged it through snow drifts, over hills and along rough roads into Sturgis.

She pawned her engagement ring for $25 to pay some men to dig a grave. It was so cold and the soil so solid that fires had to be lit on the ground for four hours before it was soft enough to dig.

After she had seen Tubbs buried, 'Poker Alice' went to the local saloon.

'I'd like to deal,' she told the owner. 'But only until I've earned $25.'

Soon she was back on her chicken farm. And the engagement ring was back on her finger.

After Tubbs's death 'Poker Alice' decided to raise sheep and hired a man named George Huckert to manage the ranch.

Times were hard and money was scarce. Huckert's wages piled up and up.

Years later 'Poker Alice' told a friend how she solved the predicament.

'You know,' she recalled, 'I owed him about $1,008 and all I had was about $50 on hand, so I got to figuring it would be cheaper to marry him than to pay him off.'

They separated soon afterwards and 'Poker Alice' resumed her second husband's name – Tubbs. The sheep ranch was a failure and she went back to the gaming tables. In 1912 she opened a gambling club which was popular with soldiers from near-by Fort Meade. Every pay-night the club was crowded as 'Poker Alice' separated the troops from their money over the card tables.

One night a bunch of drunken troopers returned to the club after closing time and demanded to be let in. 'Poker Alice' did not know whether they were after more liquor or had come to rob her. She got her gun and shouted for them to go away or she would shoot. Eventually she fired through the door to frighten them. She heard a thud outside as a trooper from Company K, Fourth Cavalry, fell dead.

At her trial 'Poker Alice' was found guilty but released by a soft-hearted judge who told her: 'I cannot find it in my heart to send a white-haired old lady to the penitentiary.'

The Army put her club out of bounds after that and she lost a lot of trade. The only thing that would have brought back business would have been to turn it into a whorehouse.

And that 'Poker Alice' would never do.

Eventually she retired for the last time and went back to her small ranch near Sturgis. She liked to wander about the country wearing a khaki drill shirt, homespun skirt and a battered old cavalry hat. She knew that the old life was behind her forever. The only thing she retained was her love for the cheroots that had become her trade mark.

Dr Noley Mumey, the Colorado historian, visited her and Alice talked of her life.

'We were all gamblers in those days,' she said. 'Some staked their claims in mines, some in goods, some in cattle, some with a pan at a stream. I took mine at a table with a deck of cards.'

Tourists often called at the ranch to see the little old lady with the slight English accent who was a real-life legend and a hang-over from the roaring days of the Old West.

It was a visiting tourist who found her bedridden and dying early in 1930.

She was rushed to hospital, but the surgeon told her at 79 she was too old to be operated on. It would be a gamble even if she was young and strong, he said.

'I've been taking gambles all my life,' the little old lady told him. 'If there's one thing I can't stand it's a fellow who bluffs out in the first round. Go ahead and operate.'

He did, and 'Poker Alice', who had won and lost more than half a million dollars in her lifetime, died on the operating table on 27th February, 1930.

CHAPTER THIRTEEN

THE PRETENDER

ON 30TH JUNE, 1934, more than ten thousand curious people gathered at San Franciso's Woodlawn Cemetery to see the re-burial of an Englishman whose extraordinary life had added colour to another era. On that day Joshua Abraham Norton, an English Jew who set himself up as 'Emperor of the United States', was re-interred with full military honours 54 years after he had died.

Joshua Abraham Norton was the second son of John Norton and his wife Sarah. Born in the East End of London on 4th February, 1819, young Joshua was taken to Grahamstown, South Africa by his family the following year. He became a colonial soldier and served in most parts of the almost unexplored Cape Province, returning to Cape Town to spend his leaves with his family who had opened a store.

Thrifty John Norton had a thriving business in Cape Town and was looking for new fields to conquer. When young Joshua came out of the army in 1844 his father put him in charge of a two-masted trading brig he was sending to Peru and Chile.

The elder Norton died shortly after Joshua returned from the trading mission which had been a roaring success. Immediately he fitted out another ship and set off for South America again, this time to Brazil. But Norton's ship was destroyed by fire in the harbour at Rio de Janeiro and all his trading stock went up in flames with it.

A few weeks later word reached Rio that gold had been found at Sutter's Fort in California and the great gold rush began. Joshua Norton was one of the first to book a passage on the German ship *Franziska* and he arrived in San Francisco on 23rd November, 1849.

Norton opened an office at 242, Montgomery Street, a street

destined to become the most prosperous and thriving business thoroughfare in the booming city. He began in a small way, dealing in coal. Soon he took a man named Robertson into partnership with him and the firm of Joshua Norton & Co. expanded their interests to deal in beef and bricks as well.

Then, in 1851, came the first of two fires which were to change his life. In this one he lost everything he owned, the partnership broke up and the Englishman was once more on his own. By borrowing from friends he started business again, this time in tea, coffee, flour and rice. By 1853 he had paid off all his debts and had $250,000 in the bank.

Then Norton decided to corner the rice market. Whenever a ship with rice came into port he was there to meet it and buy the cargo. In order to make certain that he would have a complete monopoly he was prepared to outbid any opposition just to get it into his warehouse. Two brothers who tried to break the monopoly often forced Norton to bid far above the price that rice was worth and his bank balance fell sharply.

And then, in November, 1856, came the second fire.

Norton's warehouse was gutted. He was not insured, and he was ruined. He had $15,000 in the bank but his debts totalled $55,811. Paying off what he could, Norton left San Francisco.

Where he went, what he did and with whom during the next three years is a mystery.

But on 17th September, 1859, he re-appeared again. On that day a strange and bizarre figure walked into the office of the San Francisco *Evening Bulletin* and announced that he was the Emperor of the United States.

The editor described him as 'a well-dressed and serious-looking man' which hardly fitted the extraordinary apparition which presented itself before him. It wore a dark green frock coat with gold epaulettes, bright blue trousers with a broad red stripe down each side, and a top hat with a long green ostrich feather held in place by a large red cockade. A large military sabre drooped at his side and his highly-polished black boots were neatly split open at the toes – for Joshua Norton suffered from corns.

He told the editor that he was 'Norton I, Emperor of the United

States'. And he handed the surprised man a Proclamation, neatly written in a bold copper-plate hand.

It read:

> At the peremptory request and desire of a large majority of the citizens of these United States, I, Joshua Norton, formerly of Algoa Bay, Cape of Good Hope, and now for the last 9 years and 10 months past of San Francisco, California, declare and proclaim myself Emperor of these United States; and in virtue of the authority thereby in me vested, do hereby order and direct the representatives of the different States of the Union to assemble in the Musical Hall, of this city, on the 1st day of February next, then and there to make such alterations in the existing laws of the Union as may ameliorate the evils under which the country is laboring, and thereby cause confidence to exist, both at home and abroad, in our stability and integrity.
>
> NORTON I,
> Emperor of the United States.

Because he had a sense of humour, and because he had a paper to fill, the editor printed it. But overnight he found he had a success on his hands as San Franciscans, eager for more news of the man who had overthrown the Republic of the United States with a stroke of his pen, clamoured for more news of the Emperor. It was all a great joke – except that Norton I was deadly serious.

A month later he supplied the *Bulletin* with another proclamation which said: '. . . fraud and corruption prevent a fair play and proper expression of the public voice . . . We do hereby abolish Congress and it is hereby abolished.'

When he heard from the capital at Washington that Congress was still sitting, Norton I was furious.

He stormed into the *Evening Bulletin's* office and gave the editor an edict to be printed at once.

It read:

> We do hereby Order and Direct Major General Scott, the Commander-in-Chief of our Armies, immediately on receipt of this our Decree, to proceed with a suitable force and clear the Halls of Congress.

And when this was not done he took drastic action, pro-
claiming:

> We, Norton I, by the Grace of God and the National Will,
> Emperor of the Thirty-three States and the multitude of Ter-
> ritories of the United States, do hereby DISSOLVE the Re-
> public of the United States of America.

By now Norton was becoming a fast favourite with San Franciscans. Mothers pointed him out in crowds, children ran to
touch his coat-tails and he always held their hands and spoke to
them with Imperial condescension.

It delighted him to see his loyal subjects around him.

One thing that bothered the Emperor was how to keep the
Imperial body and soul together. So he visited a jobbing printer
named Charles Murdoch and arranged for some 'Bonds of
Empire' to be printed free of charge. In return he appointed Murdoch Chancellor of the Imperial Exchequer. On each Bond was a
portrait of Norton I and the Great Seal of the State of California,
and the words 'The Imperial Government of NORTON I'.

Each Bond was hand-signed by the Emperor who promised
'to pay the holder hereof, the sum of Fifty Cents in the year
1880, with interest at 5 per cent per annum from date, the
principal and interest to be convertable, at the option of the
holder, at maturity, into 20 years' 5 per cent. Bonds, or payable
in Gold Coin'. The Bonds cost 50 cents each.

Norton also levied minor taxes on the wealthy business houses
along Montgomery Street and they all paid happily. For the
demands of the Imperial Exchequer were modest.

The Eureka Lodging House on Commercial Street became his
home for 21 years and the rent – 50 cents a day – was paid each
month by the Occidental Lodge F. and A.M. to which he had
belonged in more prosperous days.

Norton ate at all the best restaurants – free of charge – and
was not above sending food back to the kitchen with a stern
rebuke if it failed to please the Imperial palate.

He picked up two dogs, Bummer and Lazarus, and they were
his constant companions until Lazarus was poisoned after a
number of years and Bummer was kicked to death by a drunk. By
this time both Norton and his regal hounds were so famous that

when the sad news reached him Samuel Clemens – Mark Twain – reported the passing of Bummer in the columns of his *Territorial Enterprise* in Virginia City, Nevada. Emperor Norton he described as 'a lovable old humbug'. Soon Samuel Clemens was to be more famous than the Emperor. For he became known in the literary world as Mark Twain.

In 1860, with constant revolutions, counter-revolutions and French intervention keeping Mexico in a constant turmoil, Emperor Norton decided to take the matter in hand.

He declared himself 'Protector of Mexico' and published a Proclamation to that effect in which he stated: 'Mexico is entirely unfit to manage her own affairs, the country being in a constant stage of internal distraction, anarchy and civil war.'

And as the clouds of conflict loomed over America and the country headed for a civil war of their own, Norton I, became increasingly worried.

Rapidly he took command of the situation and issued the following Proclamation:

> At the request of a large majority of the citizens of the Republic, you have been directed to assemble here, this day, to ratify, alter, or reject, a proposed alteration of the form of your government. An alteration is demanded and insisted upon, or We should not have been entrusted with the authority to have called a Convention of the Nation for that object . . .

When the War Between The States flared up he hastily summoned President Abraham Lincoln of the United States and President Jefferson Davis of the Confederate States to attend a conference. Neither came so he summoned the leaders of their armies, Generals Ulysses S. Grant and Robert E. Lee. They too were otherwise engaged.

The *Evening Bulletin* had become the official Imperial mouthpiece which suited the editor well enough for Emperor Norton was a certain circulation-booster. But other papers who were less favoured by the Emperor frequently attacked him in their columns.

Angered by their jibes Norton issued another Proclamation in which he said: 'I decree that the good sense and honesty of purpose of the Nation is not to be insulted by such trash.'

All agreed that Norton was a very good Emperor. He attended a different church each week and for these occasions he wore his official, ceremonial sabre. He attended all public meetings and functions, taking for himself the most prominent place on the platform – as befitted the dignity of an Emperor. And, when he could spare the time, he attended sittings of the State Legislature in Sacramento taking copious notes in a large black book. He pressed for better street lighting, for tarred instead of cobbled streets, for a new City Hall, for a new post office and for better fire protection. He spoke out against the discriminatory laws of the time which made the evidence of San Francisco's many thousands of Chinese inadmissable in courts. And he loudly decried the immigration laws which denied entry to a man because of the colour of his skin.

He campaigned against official corruption in high places in the city and issued a Proclamation to that effect. It read:

> The Public Officials having again notoriously betrayed the confidence and trust imposed in them by a trusting people; and having shamefully disregarded the public interest and the people's welfare to feather their own nests; now, therefore, We, Norton I, Emperor of America and Protector of Mexico, do hereby order all such Officials to resign forthwith, and do declare their said offices vacant from the date hereof.
>
> Norton I, Emperor.

And in 1866, when a new water supply for the growing city was under consideration, he weighed up the facts carefully and decided that it was not the right one. His Proclamation on the matter said:

> The taxpayer is now feeling the effects of universal suffrage and the American vote: and Whereas; the fraudulent system which the politicians have engendered cannot give the taxpayer his pro-rata of the spoils, NOW, THEREFORE, We, Norton I, Dei Gratia, do hereby prohibit the Water Commissioners from signing the Spring Valley Water bill under penalty of decapitation until a sounder system shall have been adopted.
>
> Given under our hand and seal.

San Franciscans were outraged when a new policeman named Barbier arrested the Emperor as a vagrant on 21st January, 1867.

The Chief of Police had him instantly released and tendered his profuse apologies for the officer's 'unwarrantable licence in interfering with the free conduct of the Imperial Person'.

In 1869 Emperor Norton took on the Central Pacific Railroad. They had already given him a free lifetime pass to enable him to travel to and from Sacramento to listen to the proceedings of the State Legislature. But that did not stop him from issuing a Proclamation demanding that they undertake a sizeable project.

This time he chose *The Oakland Daily News* as the medium for making his wishes known. On 18th August, 1869, they published this Proclamation:

> We, Norton I, DEI GRATIA, Emperor of the United States and Protector of Mexico, do order and direct, first, that Oakland shall be the coast termination of the Central Pacific Railroad; secondly, that a suspension bridge be constructed from the improvements lately ordered by our royal decree at Oakland Point to Yerba Buena . . .

Engineers laughed at the time. But fifty years later the Golden Gate suspension bridge was built some 26 miles east of Norton's proposed bridge.

The following year the Franco-Prussian War broke out and Norton allied himself with Bismark. He wrote frequently and at length, advising on strategy. Many of his letters and proclamations were printed in German newspapers. When Prussia won, Norton was not slow to take his share of the credit.

An Imperial crisis was narrowly averted in 1878 by the farsighted editor of the *Evening Bulletin* publishing a small news item which read: 'His Majesty's full dress never-mention-'ems have lost their seat, and there is a dangerous risk of the Empire being brought into contempt.'

The San Francisco Board of Supervisors stepped in and provided the Emperor with a complete new outfit.

Wrote Robert Louis Stevenson in *The Wrecker*: 'In what other city would a harmless madman who supposed himself Emperor of the two Americas have been so fostered and encouraged? Where else would even the people of the streets have resurrected the poor soul's illusions? Where else could bankers and merchants have received his visits, cashed his checks, and submitted to his small assessments? . . . Where else, in God's Green Earth, could he have taken his pick of the restaurants, ransacked the bill of fare, and departed scatheless? They tell me he was even an exacting patron, threatening to withdraw his custom when dissatisfied.'

No person or company was too large or too small for the Emperor to consider them exempt from his attentions. And he was always the champion of the little man being pushed around by big companies or by bureaucracy – especially so when the company concerned was considered to be poaching on the Imperial preserve. Once he even took on powerful Wells, Fargo, gold shippers, bullion merchants and bankers, who had informed their agents that C. Averill, one of their former employees, was now working for a rival concern and was to be treated 'as any other employee of an opposition Express Co.' Norton considered this 'a seditious proclamation and command' distributed 'amongst the most faithful of my agents and subjects', and a trampling on the rights of Mr Averill. He immediately issued a Proclamation that 'no notice shall be paid to proclamations issued by Pretenders to my authority, ability and Regal position', and threatened to 'banish from my Kingdom' anyone who did take notice.

His annual 'End Of The Year Message' delivered on 31st December, 1879, was his last. Fittingly it ended with 'prayers of thanksgiving to Almighty God'.

At 8.15 p.m. on January 8th, 1880, Emperor Norton, on his way up California Street to attend a public meeting at the Academy of Sciences, collapsed on some steps and died. He was 61.

The *San Francisco Chronicle* headlined their story on his death: 'Le Roi est Mort.'

Another staunch supporter among the Press, the *Alta California*, wrote: 'Since he has worn the Imperial purple he has shed no blood, robbed nobody, and despoiled of the country of no one, which is more than can be said for any of his fellows in that line.'

An estimated 30,000 people saw him lying in state at the funeral parlour, and his burial at Marion Cemetery, paid for by members of the Pacific Club, cost $10,000.

In 1934 his body was removed to Woodlawn Cemetery by the

Emperor Norton Association and a square stone bearing his titles and dates was erected. After the Municipal Band had played many sombre airs, three volleys were fired over the grave by the 159th Infantry and the Last Post was sounded. Mayor Rossi then laid a wreath on the grave.

Joshua Abraham Norton had lived like an Emperor and he was buried like one.

But history has yet to decide whether the English Emperor of the United States was truly a great eccentric – or one of the smoothest confidence tricksters of all time who parlayed the people's love of the bizarre into a way of living and eating free of charge.

CHAPTER FOURTEEN

THE RAILROADER

IN THE Omaha, Nebraska, Public Library there is a glass jar. And in the jar is the scalp of an Englishman named William Thompson who found America tougher than he had anticipated.

The telegraph had gone dead precisely at 9.0 p.m. on the night of 6th August, 1867. William Thompson, telegraph operator at the isolated station of Plum Creek, Nebraska, cursed silently to himself as he trudged over to the sections men's barracks.

It was bound to be the Indians. It always was. The telegraph did not break down of its own accord. For more than a year the Cheyennes had waged a private war upon it. The telegraph line and the railroad: their two enemies. Now the workers on both travelled heavily armed.

Thompson pushed open the door of the barracks and turned the men out. He cursed the day he had left his native Hampshire to go to America. And he cursed the day he had begun working for the Union Pacific Railroad.

Picking up their guns and tools William Thompson, Sam Wallace, Jim Delahunty, John Kearn, Tim Murphy, Pat Handerhand and Pat Griswold climbed aboard a handcar and began pumping themselves down the track to find the break.

Three miles from Plum Creek station the handcar suddenly leaped into the air and crashed down the embankment spilling the seven men in all directions. Doggedly they staggered back up the incline on to the railbed. Thompson had time to see a rail prised up from its sleepers and rested across a rock before the Indians struck.

Screaming like fiends forty Cheyennes charged from the underbrush and began urging their horses up the incline firing as they came. The railroaders scattered and ran. They had lost their guns when the handcar overturned.

124

Pat Handerhand was ridden down and hacked to pieces with tomahawks; Pat Griswold ran off into the darkness with three Cheyennes hot on his tail. Wallace, Kearn, Murphy and Delahunty plunged into the brush where the Indian ponies could not follow.

A painted warrior rode at William Thompson as he raced for the comparative safety of the brush. A bullet smashed into his right arm and he staggered but ran on. The Indian urged his pony forward and swept past Thompson. His rifle swung downwards and the fleeing man spun to the ground.

Thompson was barely conscious as the Cheyenne warrior returned and sprang from his pony. He felt the Indian's fingers in his hair and then the brutal slicing of the knife as it scored a line around the top of his head. He wanted to scream but knew it would mean instant death. The pain was excruciating. He bit his lips while suppressing a scream and as the Cheyenne jerked at the hair Thompson felt as if the whole of his head was being torn away.

The Indian stood up clutching Thompson's bloody scalp and grunted in triumph. In a moment he was on his horse and racing away to join the rest of the Indians in their search for the other railroaders.

But the blood from the scalp made it slippery. Thompson, half-blinded by blood, saw it fall from the Cheyenne's fingers. The Indian whirled his horse and jumped down to retrieve his trophy from the long grass.

Suddenly a long tendril of light stabbed out into the night as a seventeen-car freight train approached round the bend. The Cheyenne stopped in his tracks.

The train hit the raised rail at twenty-five miles an hour, tipped on its side and sent up a great cloud of steam. The tender and the three leading freight cars catapulted over the engine and plunged down the embankment as the remaining cars piled up and slid from the tracks.

Fireman George Henshaw was trapped in the engine cab and scalded to death by steam. Engineer Brooks Bowers, tossed into the air as the engine tipped, was trapped in the wreckage. Conductor Kinney, riding in the rear car, was unhurt. He waited until the Indians had gathered round the shattered engine and then slipped from the train and made his way back up the tracks.

William Thompson saw the Cheyenne abandon his hunt for the lost scalp and leap astride his pony. As he rode off to join the other Indians by the train one thought was uppermost in Thompson's mind: he must regain his scalp. Painfully he began to crawl to where he had seen it fall. At last he found it in the grass. The effort had weakened him. He barely had the strength to push it inside his shirt before he blacked out.

Meanwhile Conductor Kinney had flagged down another freight train, reported the crash and had it backed up the line to Plum Creek Station.

There he found Wallace, Kearn, Murphy and Delahunty who reported the handcar wreck. They had seen Pat Handerhand go down under the Cheyenne tomahawks and presumed that Pat Griswold and William Thompson had also been killed. But an hour later Griswold dragged himself into the station almost out of his mind with pain. A bullet had shattered his hip but he had managed to crawl the three miles to safety.

News of the train wreck and Indian attack was sent to Omaha, nearly three hundred miles away, and the railroaders bedded down as best they could for the night.

The following morning, reinforced by a party of armed settlers, they hitched a flatcar in front of the engine, piled a barricade of railroad sleepers across the front of it, and set off down the line once more.

A mile from the scene of the wreck they saw a man staggering about on the tracks ahead of them.

It was William Thompson. His scalped head had turned black as the blood dried and his face was streaked with blood, sweat and tears. He babbled incoherently and waved his grisly scalp at the horrified railroaders.

They took Thompson aboard the flatcar and steamed slowly down the line to the wreck. It lay smouldering in the morning light, but it had burned brightly all night. The Indians, after pillaging the cars, had set them on fire. A few Cheyennes still remained near by. They had tied bolts of coloured cloth to their horses' tails and ridden madly around; ribbons had been plaited into manes; a barrel of whisky salvaged from the train had been broken open and most of the Indians were drunk.

Jim Delahunty, brother of Pat, dropped a warrior with a long

Clement Bothamley (*from 'The Life of Nellie C. Bailey', 1885*).

Grave of Clement Bothamley and his wife. (*Courtesy Waldo Koop.*)

Nellie Bailey (*from 'The Life of Nellie C. Bailey', 1885*).

[To face pag. 126]

Ben Thompson, gunfighter from Yorkshire. (*Denver Public Library Western Collection.*)

shot from his rifle and the Indians ran for their ponies and
rode off carrying their dead companion and such booty as they
could.

The railroaders found Engineer Brooks Bowers hanging by
one mangled leg from the engine car. He was still alive. The
Indians had found it amusing to let him hang upside down in
agony as the flames from the burning train licked around him.
It was a miracle that he was still alive.

They returned to Plum Creek with Thompson and Bowers. A
trainload of soldiers had arrived and more were being sent. The
line to Omaha was cleared and the two injured men were placed
in a special car for a frantic dash to Omaha and the nearest
doctor.

William Thompson was rational but steadfastly refused to be
parted from his scalp. He believed that it might be grafted back
on to his head. It was put into a bucket of salt water where it
lay like a drowned rat.

The train pulled into Omaha after a record run. Both men
were still alive. A huge crowd had assembled at the station.
Among them was a young Welshman named Henry M. Stanley
who, four years later would gain international fame in Africa for
asking 'Dr Livingstone, I presume?' At the time he was a reporter for the *Missouri Democrat*.

'People flocked from all parts to view the gory baldness which
came upon Thompson so suddenly,' wrote Stanley to his paper.
'The man was evidently suffering tortures and appeared weak
from loss of blood.'

Thompson was taken to the Hamilton House and Dr Pecke
and Dr R. C. Moore were sent for. They soon dashed his hopes
that his scalp could ever grow back. Their main concern was to
save his life.

Dr R. C. Moore made this report to the Second Annual Meeting of the Nebraska State Medical Society:

'William Thompson, an employee of the Union Pacific Rail
Road, was scalped by the Cheyenne Indians near Plum Creek
Station on the night of August 6, 1867. He was placed under my
care on the morning of the 8th, about 36 hours after the wounds
were inflicted.

'The scalp was entirely removed from a space measuring 9

E

inches by 7. The denuded surface extended from one inch above the left eyebrow backwards.

'There also was a severe tomahawk wound, also a slight gunshot wound through the fleshy part of the right arm. Supperation was very profuse, but the patient, being strong and in excellent health, rapidly recovered.

'He had severe neuralgic pains on the right side of the head and face, but in about three months all pain ceased and nearly the entire surface was cicatrized.'

William Thompson decided to quit his job with the Union Pacific and soon afterwards he decided to quit the United States altogether.

Before he returned to his native Hampshire he presented his scalp to Dr Moore. In later years the good doctor gave it to the Omaha Public Library where it rests today.

CHAPTER FIFTEEN

THE BIGAMIST

CLEMENT BOTHAMLEY'S family were definitely of the top
drawer. They claimed direct lineal descent from John Churchill
who became the Duke of Marlborough because of his brilliant
military successes in the Netherlands Wars. Their home in Kent
was filled with historical bric-a-brac and the family honour was
shining bright even if the family coffers were a little low in
funds.

But Clement Bothamley was the black sheep of the family. He
fell in love with a young girl called Hattie and then jilted her to
marry a woman who had private means and a rich family as well.

Two years later he met Hattie again. She had married a sea
captain called Mellick but his ship had gone down in the Indian
Ocean and she was a widow. Bothamley's marriage had produced
two children but it was far from a success. Hattie also had two
children. A month after meeting again they left her children
with her mother and Bothamley deserted his wife, bought two
tickets for the United States and sailed from Liverpool with the
girl he had jilted. They travelled as Mr and Mrs Mellick.

From New York they went to Chicago and in March, 1880,
they arrived in Newton, Kansas, posing as man and wife – they
may even have been married somewhere on the way. Bothamley
bought the old Marsh Mansion for $5,350 and settled in. They
planned to get established and then send to England for Hattie's
two children.

Newton had had its heyday as a wild and booming cattle centre
where the Texas trail herds ended their long journey north and
the beef were shipped on the hoof east on the Santa Fe Railroad.
Those were the days – nine years before Bothamley's arrival –
when Texas drovers swaggered down the streets booted and
spurred and the Town Marshal slept with a loaded shotgun by

his bed. In 1871 there had been a bloody fight in Perry Tuttle's Dance Hall which ended with five men dead and four badly wounded. It was known as 'The Newton General Massacre'.

But by 1880 the town had settled down as a centre of prairie commerce, a big stop on the Santa Fe Railroad and a pleasant town in which to bring up a family. And Hattie was pregnant.

In June she died in childbirth and the baby died with her. She was buried in the local cemetery and Clement Bothamley put up a handsome marble pillar over the grave. The town at large felt very sorry for him.

The young Englishman became a kind of recluse, living alone in the big house and drinking heavily. For a short time he went to stay with English friends, Mr and Mrs John W. Weaver, in the town and while he was with them he met briefly a young lady named Nellie Bailey who would have a profound influence on his life. They only met for a short while and later Bothamley went back to live at the Marsh Mansion and brood about his Hattie.

In 1881 he finally sold the house for $7,000 and bought a ranch near Sedgwick City, in Sedgwick County, Kansas. Soon afterwards he travelled to the town of Emporia and met up with Nellie Bailey again. Her father owned a farm at near by Halstead. Once more they parted, but two years later they were to meet again in St Louis.

And at this third meeting Bothamley persuaded her to join him at his ranch.

How much he knew of beautiful Nellie's wild background is uncertain. It seems that he must have known of at least some of it because he agreed that they could not go on living in Kansas, but would move to Texas where she was not known to the local populace whose straight-laced views would have made their relationship, even after marriage, very difficult.

She was born Nellie C. Benthusen on 19th September, 1863, at Algonquin, in McHenry County, Illinois, of Scots-German parentage and in 1871 her father had moved to Halstead, Harvey County, Kansas, with his family – there was also a son – and began to farm in the free range country. Nellie had been sent to school at Rockford Seminary in Illinois, and her unorthodox ways soon attracted a good deal of talk.

She was a remarkable striking young woman with a strong

will and a contempt for conventions. When she was sixteen she fell for Alvin Lakenside who she was later to describe as 'a firm, sober, industrious and intellectual young man'.

They were due to be married on 17th August, 1879, but the irresponsible Nellie ran away with Shannon Bailey, a wealthy Newton banker who was considerably her senior in years. They were married eight days before she should have been wed to young Lakenside and she jilted him by note.

It did not take long for Shannon Bailey to become tired of his young wife and he gave her $4,000 to get out of his life. Nellie left. It is unlikely that there was a divorce.

Nellie met Clement Bothamley soon afterwards at the Weavers' home in Newton. She was immediately impressed with the young man and heard of his recent bereavement from the lovely Hattie.

She described him later as 'a very handsome man, about twenty-eight years of age', and said that 'he possessed fine business qualifications, and was highly intellectual, but his face bore unmistakable marks of dissipation'.

Nellie and Bothamley did not meet again for a year and during that time she went to eastern Kansas to try her luck as an actress with a stage troupe. They went east to New York and then travelled to Wisconsin. During that time she met Robert Reese, a handsome young actor in her theatrical company, and one night after a party at Washeuk, Wisconsin, she accepted a dare from him to go to the home of a justice of the peace and get married. There was no certificate or certain legality in the ceremony but it was accepted as legitimate. Reese and Nellie soon parted.

Then she met Clement Bothamley again in St Louis.

Nellie knew that she could not return to Kansas where she was known and just set up home with Bothamley. She was calling herself Nellie Bailey, having retained Shannon Bailey's surname, but Bothamley's ranch was reasonably near to Newton and there would have been talk. Shannon had gone to Canada and Nellie claimed later that she had heard that he was dead. Also, her family were still living at Halstead and might also hear about her return to the State. She knew that they would not approve of her living with the Englishman, and so it was decided that the ranch would be sold and that they would marry and start afresh in Texas. Then, and only then, would she tell the family about the marriage and she would take Bothamley to meet them. In the meantime she would live with him at the ranch posing as his sister Sarah, just arrived from England.

The plan worked well enough. They reached the ranch in July, 1883, and Bothamley had a lot of business to clear up in the county and was too busy to take on any social engagements. Whenever Nellie ventured out of doors she wore a big hat, dark glasses and a heavy white veil and Bothamley explained to his ranch hands that his sister was worried about spoiling her beautiful peaches-and-cream English complexion in the harsh Kansas sun.

Bothamley was a sick man, suffering badly from rheumatism and sciatica and Nellie herself made many of the arrangements for the sale of the property. She discovered that he was considerably more wealthy than she had at first thought and was delighted when he gave her some Churchill family diamonds and a delicately-worked little locket containing a hand-painted miniature of Lady Churchill.

Sometimes the Englishman was bed-ridden, but most of the time he managed to drag himself around the ranch and assist with the plans for the move to Texas.

Nellie commented later that he 'possessed so much of the English stubbornness that he generally accomplished whatever he undertook'.

A wagon was fixed up with a wooden hood, rather like a gypsy caravan, in which they would make the trip to Texas and Bothamley bought a flock of two thousand two hundred sheep to drive with them and use as the basis of a sheep empire which he would carve out of the north Texas range country. He also hoped that the dry climate would help his rheumatism. Two men – 15-year-old Wesley Vetter and William Dodson – were hired to act as sheep drovers.

On 21st August, 1883, the wagon and sheep moved off from the Sedgewick ranch bound for Texas.

They moved slowly, allowing the sheep to graze as they went along and on the night of 7th October, 1883, they were camped at Hackleberry Creek in Garfield County, some six miles from the settlement of Waukomis.

Vetter and Dodson, the herders, were bedded down with the sheep some distance from the wagon where Bothamley and Nellie Bailey slept.

About three in the morning there was a shot which awakened the herders but they took little notice of it. Then, two hours later, just after dawn, they heard Nellie – they knew her as Sarah Bothamley – screaming for them to hurry to the wagon.

The two men looked inside but Nellie refused to enter.

Clement Bothamley lay on his back with a bullet hole in his head close to the right eye.

Sobbing, Nellie told the herders that he had killed himself. A .45 calibre Colt revolver lay on the bed and one shot had been fired from it.

At about the same time two local ranchers, Ralph Collins and J. W. C. Donaldson, rode up. They had been camping on the prairie overnight and were on their way home. Collins raced into Waukomis to summon help and a posse rode out headed by Abe Rhodes.

He scouted around and found a pillow with the ticking saturated with blood lying near a creek some distance from the wagon. There was a hole in the case about the size of a man's thumb – or a .45 calibre bullet. He also noted that the bullet hole in Bothamley's head appeared to have ranged downwards – a circumstance which he considered might rule out suicide.

The body was taken to the Skeleton Ranch and a coffin was hastily made from dry goods boxes. Collins and Donaldson helped prepare the body for burial and O. G. Wells, a Sioux Indian, and Anderson Hans dug the grave. Aside from the weeping Nellie, eleven men and four women attended the funeral, one of the first recorded in that section of the country.

After the burial Nellie, Dodson and Vetter rode back to the wagon, rounded up the sheep and moved Southeast, carrying on towards Texas.

Meanwhile Abe Rhodes reported his suspicions to Pat. D. Terrill, a United States Government Agent who worked under U.S. Commissioner J. F. Sherman at Wichita. The Commissioner notified Deputy United States Marshal Cash Hollister at Caldwell, Kansas, and he took two men and a zinc coffin and set out after Nellie and the wagon. One of his possemen was Henry Newton Brown, City Marshal of Caldwell, an apparently reformed gunfighter who had once ridden stirrup to stirrup with Billy the Kid in New Mexico but had quit him to become first a policeman in Tascosa, Texas, and then a full-time lawman in Caldwell. The other man was Ben Wheeler, also a reformed gunfighter, who was Assistant Marshal under Brown.

The lawmen caught up with Nellie Bailey and her herders and turned them back towards the Skeleton Ranch. Hollister had Clement Bothamley's remains dug up and encased in the zinc box and then set off for Caldwell with his prisoners. From there they went to Wichita where the body was examined by Commissioner Sherman and then sent to Newton where it was buried beside Hattie Mellick and her baby.

The Wichita *Eagle* had editorialised that 'the affair has every appearance of a dark and bloody deed' and drew attention to the fact that Nellie Bailey had in her possession a letter addressed to John C. Johnson, Registrar of Deeds at Newton.

U.S. Commissioner Sherman also thought this was significant, especially when he discovered that it contained notations that if anything happened to Bothamley all his property, including the family jewellery, passed to Nellie Bailey.

He acquitted William Dodson of complicity in the suspected crime but held him on bail of $500 to appear at the trial. Nellie Bailey went back to the Wichita jail and in mid-November was taken to the State capital of Topeka by Deputy U.S. Marshal Wade. There she was visited by Alvin Lakenside, the man she had jilted to run away with Shannon Bailey.

On 15th November there was a new slant to the case when Robert Reese arrived in Wichita and announced that he was going to sue Nellie for divorce, claiming that she had married him against his will. The local citizens found this highly amusing and made much of it.

A reporter on the *Eagle* described Nellie as 'the dark eyed, trim, handsome young woman, the fire of whose nature so surely enwraps all with whom she comes in contact . . . but whose face and eyes have persuaded everybody of her innocence excepting the U.S. Attorney, her prosecutor'.

In the meantime the very strong British-American Association in Kansas – of which Clement Bothamley had been a member – had taken an interest in the case and a man named Phillips, who lived in Newton and was the head of the Association, was asked by Commissioner Sherman to handle the probate side of Bothamley's estate. He contacted the British Ambassador in Washington and through him traced a brother living in Florida and another in Ontario, Canada. Pat Terrill, the U.S. Government Agent, was also given instructions to handle the case for Her Majesty's Government and to keep the British Ambassador fully informed.

Nellie Bailey was held in custody for sixteen months before she appeared for trial before Judge Foster at Wichita. The case had attracted considerable nation-wide attention and the courtroom was too small. So the trial was held instead in the Opera House. Nellie's beauty had swayed a good number of heads and the revelation in Fox's scurrilous and widely-read *Police Gazette* that Nellie had put away two men for their money before she even met Bothamley added a juicy titbit for the crowd.

Some of the best legal talent in Kansas was represented. The defence lawyers were led by W. E. Stanley of Wichita, who later became Governor of Kansas. He was assisted by Joe W. Andy, later a United States Attorney, and Thomas B. Wall, later a prominent district judge. The prosecution was handled by Colonel James R. Hallowell, a famous figure in early Kansas legal circles, and Charles Hutton. In all eighty-two witnesses were subpoenaed, but not all of them were able to appear in court.

Caldwell's up-and-coming lawmen Henry Brown and Ben Wheeler had reverted to their old habits of outlawry on 1st May, 1884, and had held up the bank at Medicine Lodge, Kansas. They had escaped, been captured and killed the same night by vigilantes. Deputy U.S. Marshal Cash Hollister, who had made the actual arrest of Nellie Bailey, had been killed by an outlaw in the line of duty at Hunnewell, Kansas.

The trial opened on 15th January, 1885.

Prosecution witness Captain R. M. Curtis of the Federal Prison at Topeka testified that Nellie Bailey had given nothing but trouble during her stay in the jail there. He spoke of her tantrums, her hysteria and her profanity and painted a very different picture of her from the demure young woman in sedate black who sat at the table in the improvised court room on trial for her life.

United States Agent Pat Terrill said that the bullet which had killed Bothamley had been fired from behind and had come out above his eye. He demonstrated that it would be very nearly impossible for a man to hold and fire a gun in such a position – especially a man with rheumatism.

Various people who had been at the Skeleton Ranch, where Bothamley was first buried, testified on Nellie's behaviour there and said that while she did some weeping she did not seem over-concerned about the death of the Englishman.

There the prosecution rested its case.

The defence lawyers started by putting character witnesses on the stand, but the first three were women with whom Nellie had lodged at different times and in different places and each admitted under the State's cross-examination that they had been forced to ask her to leave because of her flagrant behaviour with various men.

Doctor H. H. Dwight, who had treated the dead man for rheumatism on several occasions, testified: 'I did not consider Bothamley's mental condition sane. He used opiates, and he repeatedly asked me to take his revolver and shoot him, or give him something to put him out of the way. If he thought that he would never get well, he said he would put himself out of the way, as he had suffered so long.'

Miss Nancy Hull, who lived with Doctor Dwight, testified that Bothamley had had a revolver several times when he had been with the doctor and was always 'talking about putting a bullet through his head'. She said that 'his joints were swollen and he suffered a great deal'.

John W. Weaver testified that Bothamley had lived at his home in Newton between July, 1880, a month after Hattie's death, and February, 1881, and that Nellie Bailey had first met Bothamley in the house.

William Dodson, who had nearly stood in the dock with Nellie, testified on the condition of the inside of the wagon where Bothamley was lying dead. 'His left hand was on his breast,' he said. 'His right hand was raised and the revolver was lying on the bed near his hand. The revolver was stained with blood.'

Nellie's 'husband' Robert Reese also testified, but by this time he had put aside thoughts of divorce and treated the matter very lightly. He said that their 'marriage' had been contracted for fun. 'We did not intend it to be real, and we were never serious, as I knew Nellie did not care for me,' he said. 'I never lived with Nellie, nor considered her my wife. It was only a sham and done to spite other parties who were jealous of me.'

Wesley Vetter, one of the drovers, testified that he had worked for Bothamley briefly in November, 1882, and then from May, 1883, until his death. He said that he had once seen the Englishman put a gun to his head when he was suffering agonies from rheumatic pains, but that Nellie Bailey had snatched it away from him. Bothamley had been angry and had told her 'Give me that pistol, and I'll kill myself.'

Nellie's testimony on her own behalf clinched the jury's decision.

She used her brief acting experience to advantage, crying, shouting accusations which could not be countered or just sitting looking crestfallen. She claimed that Deputy United States Marshal Cash Hollister had promised Caldwell's Assistant Marshal Ben Wheeler $50 to give false testimony against her. Both men were dead so it could not be refuted. She claimed that she had lent Bothamley money for the purchase of the sheep and that he had signed over his property to her as surety for the loan.

Then defence attorney Stanley came up with his number one question.

'Did you kill Clement Bothamley?' he asked her point-blank.

'Kill him?' Nellie said softly. 'Kill the man I loved, the man I gave everything I possessed . . . kill Clement . . . Oh, God, no . . . no . . . no!'

She broke into sobs and was unable to continue her testimony for some minutes.

The defence winding up was a good old fashioned tear-jerker and whatever the prosecution could say made little impression on the jury. Their minds were already made up.

It took them just fifteen minutes to find Nellie Bailey not guilty.

She threw a celebration party that night and the following morning took a train to Kansas City. There she told her story to a woman writer who set it down and it was published in book form. Proceeds from the sale – and it ran into several editions, so great was the public interest in the case – paid Nellie's bills and gave her some cash to spare.

She married a man from one of the far Western States and went back to his home. She was still alive in 1933.

CHAPTER SIXTEEN

THE GUNFIGHTER

WILLIAM BARCLAY 'BAT' MASTERSON, old time lawman and gunfighter of no mean ability, thought highly of Ben Thompson's prowess with a six-shooter.

'It is doubtful if in his lifetime there was another man living who equalled him with a pistol in a life-and-death struggle,' Masterson said looking back at the lawless frontier era. 'Thompson in the first place possessed a much higher order of intelligence than the average man-killer of his time. He was absolutely without fear and his nerves were those of the finest steel. He shot at an adversary with the same precision and deliberation that he shot at a target. A past master in the use of the pistol, his aim was as true as his nerves were strong and steady.'

Masterson rated Thompson high on his list of the big-time gunfighters – a fraternity to which he, too, belonged – naming him the equal or better of Wyatt Earp, 'Wild Bill' Hickok, Bill Tilghman, Charlie Bassett, Jim Curry, Luke Short and Clay Allison.

'Little doubt exists in my mind that Thompson would have been the winner of any fight between these men,' he wrote.

Ben Thompson was born on 11th November, 1842, at Knottingly in the West Riding of Yorkshire. He had a younger brother, Billy, who was to cause him plenty of trouble, and also a sister and in 1851 their printer father took the whole family to Austin, Texas. There the young male Thompsons grew into wild boys and gradually into even wilder men.

At the outbreak of the American Civil War young Ben, only 19 years old, joined the Confederate Army. Behind him was the killing, with a Bowie knife, of a Frenchman in New Orleans and several minor tiffs with the local law for barely legal scrapes. But he was no sooner in the Army then he fell foul of authority once

more and skipped out leaving a Sergeant and a Lieutenant dead
on the floor of the barrack room.

He headed for the Mexican border and crossed it to offer
his restless gun to the French who were vainly trying to keep
the Austrian Archduke Maximillian on the throne of Mexico.
Like the Confederacy it was a lost cause but one which Ben
Thompson served to the best of his ability.

After the war he recrossed the border and became a gambler
in San Antonio, Texas, and by 1868 he was in trouble again for
shooting a man. It drew him a term in the State Penitentiary at
Huntsville.

When he came out in 1870 Thompson swore that no other
prison would ever hold him.

He returned home and collected his brother Billy before leaving for Kansas and the wide-open railhead towns to which Texans
drove vast herds of cattle for sale and shipment to a beef-hungry
East.

In 1871 Abilene, Kansas, was the railhead town. The marshal
was the fabled 'Wild Bill' Hickok, probably the fastest man with
a gun on the frontier at that time.

Ben Thompson and his partner Phil Coe opened the Bull's
Head Saloon which rapidly became a popular resort for Texans.
There was ill-feeling between the marshal and the Thompson-
Coe partnership but Ben was not in town when it came to a head.

He went to Kansas City to meet his wife Catherine, and son,
and when riding in a buggy the horse ran away and they were
thrown out. All three suffered broken limbs.

It was while he was recovering that Ben heard that Hickok and
Coe had shot it out and that Coe was dead.

After Abilene, Ben and his brother Billy moved on to Ellsworth, Kansas.

Together they ran a gambling table in the back room of Joe
Brennan's saloon.

But again the chain of killings that was to drive Ben from one
frontier town to another, broke their good luck.

In a brawl on 15th August, 1873, Billy grabbed Ben's fine
English-made shotgun and killed the Ellsworth Sheriff, Chauncey
Whitney.

Ben put Billy on a fast horse out of town and then held off

the local law officers until he thought Billy was far enough away to be clear of any pursuit.

He was fined $25 for disturbing the peace.

Ben went back to Texas and began a lucrative period in which he separated soldiers from their pay at Fort Elliott in the Texas Panhandle country.

In 1875 'Bat' Masterson, then a young man on the very brink of his career as one of the most famous lawmen in the West, was an Army scout working out of the fort.

He fell in love with Mollie Brennan, a dance hall girl, and might even have married her if her former boyfriend, an Army corporal named King, had not objected.

King warned 'Bat' several times to stay away from Mollie and then one night when he saw them together he went into action.

Snatching his gun from its holster he fired at 'Bat'. Instead he killed Mollie. A second shot hit Masterson in the thigh.

But as he fell 'Bat' grabbed his own gun and killed King with one bullet.

As the corporal's friends moved in to finish Masterson, a cold voice halted them in their tracks.

They swung round to see Ben Thompson crouched on top of a gambling table with two guns out.

'Just go back to camp boys and you'll be quite safe,' he told them. 'That was a straight fight. King got what he asked for so there's no need for you to trouble yourselves.'

The troopers left muttering and in that second a lifelong friendship was born between the lawman-to-be and the Yorkshire gambler.

In 1878, when the railroad war between the Santa Fe and the Denver and Rio Grande broke out over the right of way through Royal Gorge, Colorado, Thompson was in Dodge City and immediately joined the gang of gunfighters recruited by the Santa Fe. Another man who went along was 'Bat' Masterson.

After the almost bloodless railroad war Ben returned to Texas and settled in Austin. But a quiet town is no place for a gunfighting, high spirited marshal.

Ben began drinking heavily and liked to shoot at the top hats of salesmen from the East as they walked the dusty streets of

Austin. When this palled he shot up saloons. He always paid for the damage when he was sober, and, as nobody was ever hurt, few objected.

Billy Thompson got himself into a gunfight in Ogallala, Nebraska, in the middle of 1880 and Ben asked 'Bat' Masterson if he would go and extricate Billy from the clutches of the local law. Masterson made the trip and carried the wounded Billy back to Dodge City.

Ben knew that he lived a dangerous and precarious life and that it would probably end violently.

'Sooner or later a gambler meets an untimely death, if not from the pistol, then from fatal disease contracted by dissipation and exposure consequent on such life,' he told his friend Colonel Buck Walton one day. 'Every time a man sits down at a table to gamble he takes his life in his hands. Fatal difficulties arise from cause or no cause; men are killed in their own quarrels and in those of others. I have a son, and I would rather follow him to the grave than see him contract the habit of gambling. Yet I continue in that way of life; but so help me God, I never have and never will assist, encourage, or influence any youth or man to engage in this hell-earning business, which I will probably follow until I am dead.'

They were prophetic words and Thompson was about to embark unknowingly on a chain of events which would lead to his death because of the same gambling.

Meanwhile he carried on his drunken sprees in Austin – but the presentiment of death was with him.

Jim Long, old-time resident of the city used to tell of the day that Thompson bought a tombstone.

'I remember the circumstances well,' Long said. 'In those days a tombstone peddler named Luke Watts travelled over that part of Texas in a one-horse covered wagon. He carried a few samples of tombstones with him and took orders for them among the people in the different communities. This fellow Watts was a pretty good sculptor and if a buyer of a slab wanted some words cut on it, Watts did the work right on the spot.

'In the early days nearly every man "on the road" gambled and Luke Watts was no exception to the rule. One day he drove into Austin from San Antonio. He had taken some good orders at New Braunfels, San Marcos and other places along the route and had collected on some of his previous sales.

'He had quite a bunch of money in his pocket, and no sooner had he put his horse and wagon in the wagon yard than he headed for the Iron Front Saloon. He set them up for the crowd at the bar and then headed upstairs to the gambling room. He invested in chips and began to play.

'Soon Ben Thompson showed up and sat in on the game. Thompson was feeling pretty good and he jollied Watts about selling tombstones and making a living off dead people and that sort of thing. Watts knew Thompson for a gunfighter, but he came back at him good and strong.

' "Ben, you will be took off sudden one of these days and I may not be round just at the time to sell a tombstone to ornament your grave," he said. "You had better order one from me now."

' "A wooden board is about all I need," replied Ben with a laugh.

'The game continued and Watts was a steady loser. Finally, about midnight, he started to get up.

' "Boys, I'm cleaned out," he said.

' "Hold on there. How much are them tombstones of yours worth?" asked Thompson.

'Watts resumed his seat and looked across at Ben.

' "It depends on what kind of a stone it is," he answered.

' "I don't want no cheap monument," Ben declared. "Have you got any that are made out of marble?"

' "I have got as fine a marble slab in my wagon as you can find south of St Louis," Watts replied.

' "How much is it worth?"

' "Not a cent less than $200, which is cheap considering that it is a long way from the quarries."

' "Put that tombstone in the pot against my $200 and I will play you to win or lose," Thompson said.

' "Agreed," said Watts.

' "Bring the monument up here. I want to see it first," Ben told the pedler.

'Watts went down to the wagon yard, hitched up his horse and wagon and headed up to the front of the saloon. It was then

about two o'clock in the morning. With the aid of porters around
the place he carried the heavy stone up the stairs and set it down
alongside Ben Thompson. Ben looked it over carefully and ex-
pressed himself as satisfied with it. The game began and in a
short time Ben won the pot, including the tombstone. Watts was
unconcerned over his loss.

' "Better let me carve the inscription on it now," he said to
Ben.

' "No, you can wait until I have done something that will give
you the subject for a fitting epitaph," Thompson said.

'The tombstone occupied the centre of the gambling room for
several days and attracted much attention. Finally it was removed
on Thompson's order.'

On one of his visits to another favourite drinking place, The
Senate Saloon, Thompson had a brief run-in with the proprietor,
a hot-tempered Irishman named Mark Wilson. Just to show that
he was annoyed Thompson put a shot through the chandelier as
he was leaving.

Several days later he got word that Wilson was putting it
around town that he had run Thompson out of the saloon and
warned him not to come back. It was very much to Thompson's
liking.

On Christmas Eve, 1880, he paid a visit to The Senate and
stood drinking at the bar. Mark Wilson suddenly appeared on a
gallery with a shotgun in his hand and blasted both barrels at
Thompson. They missed, but Ben's gun was out and shooting.
His first bullet caught Wilson in the chest and toppled him from
the gallery. Three more bullets slammed into his falling body.

Suddenly there was a shot from behind Thompson. The bullet
plucked at his coat as it passed through. He spun round and
saw the barman, Mathews, holding a Winchester rifle. Matthews
ducked as Thompson turned but the gunfighter, guessing his
enemy's position behind the polished mahogany bar, fired through
the woodwork. The bullet caught Matthews in the mouth.

Thompson was acquitted at the trial and soon afterwards ran
for the office of Chief of Police. He won and a change came over
him. He stopped drinking so heavily and made a genuine attempt
to settle his own life and bring law and order to Austin.

He was highly thought of in many parts of Texas.

'Ben Thompson was a gambler, but he was my friend and an honest man,' recalled W. T. Jackson of Dallas. 'I would have trusted him with fifty thousand dollars of my money, and would have gotten it back to the last penny. I remember that Ben had a fine black mule which he rode on the streets of San Antonio. On the mule was a fifteen-hundred dollar saddle, hand-made and hand-carved, with a solid silver, jewelled horn. The saddle almost covered the mule's back, but the mule held a high head and carried Ben with an air of great pride. Ben himself had killed a lot of men in his life, but I never heard him brag about one such act. If he told you a thing was the truth you could depend on it. Nobody to my knowledge ever called Ben a crook, or proved him one.'

On a trip to San Antonio during the early part of 1882 Chief of Police Thompson called on his old friend Jack Harris who had been in the service of the Confederate States with him. Harris was not about when Thompson arrived at his friend's Vaudeville Theatre so he settled down to play a few quiet rounds of cards with one of the house dealers.

He lost heavily and decided that he was being cheated. By the time his losses reached $500 he had had enough. Harris arrived at the same moment. Thompson remarked that he had been cheated and that Harris could whistle for the money. It created some feeling but Harris contented himself with warning Thompson to leave and not to come back.

Soon afterwards Thompson, busy going about his Police duties in Austin, learned that Harris was boasting how he had backed down the great Ben Thompson.

It was the Mark Wilson situation all over again.

Thompson took a train to San Antonio and went looking for Jack Harris on 11th June. As he approached the Vaudeville Theatre he suddenly saw his former friend hiding, he thought, behind a Venetian blind with a shotgun in his hands. Enough of him was exposed to allow Thompson a good shot. He drew his gun and killed Jack Harris where he crouched in ambush.

He was found not guilty of murder but decided to resign his job as Chief of Police in Austin. Soon afterwards he began to slip back into his heavy drinking habits, and at the same time he formed a new friendship with John King Fisher, an ex-outlaw who had given Texas Ranger Captain McNelly plenty of trouble until he reformed after a jail sentence. Fisher, when he became friendly with Thompson, was Deputy Sheriff of Uvalde County.

On 11th March, 1884, Ben Thompson and King Fisher travelled to San Antonio to see a performance of *East Lynne* at the Turner Hall and afterwards they were in the mood for further entertainment.

The Vaudeville Theatre of the late Jack Harris and his partners Joe Foster and Billy Sims seemed to be an obvious choice as they specialised in shows featuring semi-nude girls. The two gunfighters wandered over there around the middle of the evening.

They occupied a box at the theatre and spent some time talking to Billy Sims. Joe Foster was not about. When they were due to leave Thompson noticed Foster drinking at the bar. He wanted to shake hands and make up the differences which had divided them over the killing of Harris but Foster was in an ill-temper and refused to be friendly.

Thompson, Fisher, Sims, Foster and the theatre policeman Jacob Coy were talking on some stairs when Foster suddenly jumped back.

The theatre exploded into a roar of sound as concealed guns were fired at Thompson and Fisher. They both went down with their own pistols still in their holsters. In the pandemonium Foster tried to draw his own pistol, but caught the hammer in his clothing and shot himself in the leg.

Thompson and Fisher were dead. The English gunfighter had eight bullets in his body, any one of five of them would have been fatal. King Fisher lay crumpled beside him with five bullets in him. Joe Foster was clutching his injured leg and bleeding profusely. He would die eleven days later.

Friends arrived the following day and King Fisher's body was taken to his home. Billy Thompson, the troublesome younger brother, rushed over to take Ben's body back to Austin.

A ballistics expert found that the bullets in his corpse were from Winchester rifles, but nobody was ever charged with the murder – or assassination – of Thompson or Fisher.

Old timers who were in the know said that cattle king Seth Mabry had been planning to see an end to Thompson, and those even more in the know named gamblers Canada Bill and Jim McLaughlin, both of them house dealers for Joe Foster, and Harry Tremaine, a Jewish actor from England, as the killers.

Ben Thompson had been right in what he said about men being killed in their own quarrels and in the quarrels of others. He had died in his own dispute and King Fisher had died with him.

It seems that nobody remembered that he had bought a tombstone from Luke Watts. At any rate it was not erected over his grave. For, many years later, when the building which had housed the Iron Door Saloon was pulled down, the marble monument that Ben had bought was found, just as he had purchased it — and still without the inscription.

CHAPTER SEVENTEEN

THE TEACHER

THE fire was spreading towards the bridge when Dr John Edward Richards went below decks with a gun in his hand. He walked among the mutineers and soon had them whipped into an efficient fire-fighting unit. There was nothing he could do for the ship's captain whom they had killed just before the fire broke out.

The ship that limped into Galveston, Texas, in mid-1857 was a far cry from the spanking clipper that had left Liverpool a few weeks before. Dr Richards turned her over to the agents and left the mutinous crew to fend for themselves as best they could. He had his own problems to attend to.

He set up in business in the little town of Brownsville, Texas, and began a new life for his wife Mary and their three children – Reuben, 14, Mary, 10, and Edward, 8. But it did not last long. Dr Richards was killed by a Comanche war party while riding back from attending a patient. Soon afterwards his wife died of yellow fever and the three children were left orphaned in a strange land.

The British Consul in Galveston heard of their plight and arranged for them to be looked after. Reuben and Edward were taken in by a family named Primm and Mary was put in a convent while the British Government was informed. Lord Salisbury, who had been a personal friend of Dr Richards, arranged for them to be made wards of court and sent a man to take them back to England.

But when the agent arrived he found that the boys had run away from the Primms and could not be traced. He returned to England with Mary and she was put in the care of one of her father's old colleagues, a Dr Bailey of St Aden's College, Southampton. She was well-educated and spent time travelling in Germany, France and Spain. For a short while she worked as a lin-

148

guist and did translations for the writers Tennyson and Ruskin and for Prime Minister Benjamin Disraeli.

But all the time she wondered about her lost brothers and at the age of twenty-five, in 1872, she said goodbye to Dr Bailey and sailed for Galveston once more. It took her a year of patient questioning in a score of frontier towns before she got her first lead. She was running low on funds, had covered hundreds of miles in stage coaches and had nearly run out of hope when she heard about the Englishman known as Don Ricardo who had abducted the daughter of Don Felix Hernandez in Mexico and taken her to live at his ranch at Yselta, Texas.

Mary Richards met her brother Reuben in El Paso, Texas, early in 1873. He and his Mexican wife had raised a fine family of four girls and four boys. He was a prosperous rancher, liked by everyone and even forgiven by his father-in-law. He told Mary that brother Edward was ranching in the Matamoras area and that he, too, was successful.

Now that she had found her family again, Mary Richards settled down to making something out of her own life. She heard that a school had been built in the mining town of Silver City, New Mexico. She took a stage to the town and applied for the job. In mid-1873 she became the first schoolmistress.

One of her pupils was a scrawny lad named Henry McCarty who was to rise to fame and notoriety in New Mexico as Billy the Kid. He was about thirteen years old at the time and lived with his mother Catherine, brother Joe and step-father William Henry Harrison Antrim. The Antrims had not been in Silver City for long. They had only been married for a few months and had moved from Santa Fe. Catherine Antrim had been Mrs Catherine McCarty, late of New York and Kansas, when Antrim had married her in Santa Fe in March that year. He had taken a job in the mines at Silver City and she ran a boarding house in town.

The story of Mary Richards and her soon-to-become-infamous pupil comes from her daughter, Mrs Patience Glennon.

'Mother told me that Billy (they called him Henry then) was a scrawny little fellow with delicate hands and an artistic nature, and that he was always quite willing to help with the chores around the school-house,' Mrs Glennon said in 1960. 'He was no more of a problem in school than any other boy growing up in a mining camp.

'They grew quite fond of each other, as a matter of fact, and my mother has told me how Billy even thought that he must be related to her. He thought this because they were both ambidextrous. My mother could write equally well with either hand, and so could Billy. He noted this and used to say to my mother that he was sure they were related because she was the only other person he ever had seen, besides himself, who could do things equally well with either hand.'

Catherine McCarty-Antrim, died in September, 1874, and the embryo Billy the Kid was put in the Star Hotel along with his brother Joe. Their stepfather lived out at the mine most of the time and asked the Truesdales, who owned the hotel, to keep an eye on his boys.

Mary Richards married Canadian millwright Daniel Casey and went to live at the Knight Ranch, some fifteen miles southwest of Silver City.

Says Mrs Glennon: 'It was about this time that Billy got into the only trouble that we knew him to be in in Silver City. His mother kept boarders and I think some of them left a trunk of women's clothes, I am not sure about this, but at any rate Billy and another boy got into some women's clothes and were parading up and down the streets of Silver City dressed up like women.

'Silver City had a strict law about this and they were arrested. This little child was thrown in jail with all these bullies and thieves and cut-throats and he managed to crawl out through a chimney and make his escape.'

She is slightly mistaken in this as Billy's mother was dead by then, but Billy certainly was involved in an incident with clothes and was jailed. He was arrested in September, 1876, for stealing clothes from two Chinese laundrymen.

According to Chauncey O. Truesdale, whose parents owned the Star Hotel where Billy lived, the young thief fled to the mines where his stepfather Antrim was working and told him about the stealing and his jail-break. Antrim gave him all the money he had on him and told him he had better leave the area.

Says Mrs Glennon: 'Mother told me how he showed up at

the Knight Ranch and told her what had happened. She and Mrs Knight put him up in the barn and brought him food for a couple of days and they tried to reason with him. They advised him to go back to Silver City and give himself up, that the penalty for what he had done was in no way as harsh as would be the life he would live in hiding. He agreed to return to Silver City and they loaned him a horse to go back on.

'But he was afraid to be put back in jail and he went in the opposite direction as soon as he was out of their sight. He went to Arizona, my mother learned later.'

The movements of Billy the Kid are vague for the next twelve months. Ash Upson, who helped the sheriff who killed the Kid in 1881 to write a book, said that Billy went to Arizona with a mysterious partner known only as 'Alias'. They killed three peaceful Indians for their horses and later the Kid was involved in a fight with Apaches. It is a documented fact that in August, 1877, the Kid was at Camp Grant, Arizona, where he killed a man named 'Windy' Cahill and made good his escape.

In the meantime Mary Richards and her husband had moved from Silver City to Georgetown, New Mexico. People knew about the young desperado who was now called Billy the Kid and his activities were closely followed.

Late in 1877 Billy the Kid rode across the line from Arizona with a murder charge hanging over his head.

Says Mrs Glennon: 'The next and last time mother saw Billy was when he came riding into Georgetown on a fine grey horse. By this time he was notorious, but he was in a fit of despondency. He told my mother that he had been down on the Mimbres visiting with his brother Joe, and that they both had tears in their eyes as he kissed his brother and told him this would probably be the last time he ever would see him.

'He showed my mother his fine horse, knowing that she was a fine horsewoman and loved animals, and he explained that he had gotten it from an Apache on the Mimbres. He had shot the Indian and took the horse.

'He told my mother that he needed money, that he would not kid her by asking to borrow some, for he'd probably never see her again. He asked if she would give him some money. My mother gave him all the cash she had in the house, voluntarily, and Billy stayed on the rest of the day, talking with mother and telling about his experiences. Along toward evening he took off.

'My father came home later that night and was all excited.

'He said to mother: "Do you know that that no-account Billy the Kid is on the loose around here? I heard that he was seen riding towards Georgetown. I wonder what that rascal is up to?"

'My mother said: "Yes, I know. He was here all day, but he is gone and won't be back. I gave him what money I had to get on with. The poor boy."

'Mother never told me what my father said then.'

Mary Richards never saw her erring pupil again. She stayed on Georgetown with her husband and raised a family of six – three girls, Patience, Edith and Blanch, and three boys, John, Simon and Daniel.

Billy the Kid just kept riding until he came to Lincoln County, New Mexico. There he stopped. And there he committed his most famous crimes.

CHAPTER EIGHTEEN

THE OPPORTUNIST

THE young Englishman sat at his desk writing home by the light of a kerosene lamp.

He wrote of his new-found friends in the rough frontier village of Lincoln, New Mexico. He wrote of his hopes, his dreams and of the great opportunities for becoming wealthy that the open spaces afforded.

'In time I intend to have fifty cents of every dollar that is made in the county by anyone,' he wrote enthusiastically. He dated his letter 27th April, 1877, addressed it in a prim copper-plate hand to his father in London.

John Henry Tunstall was born on 6th March, 1853, at 14, Liscombes Cottages, Dalston, in Hackney, then on the outskirts of London. His father was a commercial traveller at the time, but he was a successful one and the four Tunstall children grew up in comfort. Emily was the eldest, then came John and later two other sisters, Mabel and Lillian.

The elder Tunstall soon branched out and established a mercantile business. Later he took on partners and established a branch of the business in Victoria, British Columbia. And it was to British Columbia that young John was sent to get his first grounding in the business which his fond father hoped he would one day take over. He sailed for Victoria on 20th August, 1872, and arrived just over a month later crossing overland from New York.

He was nineteen, a young man brimming over with dreams of great wealth, slightly pompous, but likeable for all that.

Young Tunstall got on well with every member of the firm – except the one that mattered. For his father's partner and young Tunstall disliked each other on sight. Feelings deepened to hatred and after a little more than two years Tunstall could stand it no longer and left the firm to head south for the United States. He wandered about taking odd jobs when he felt like it, spending his father's monthly allowance frugally, but nevertheless meeting the 'right' people from California's legislature, the rich ranchers, the wealthy sheepmen, the prominent tycoons.

One of the 'right' people he met was Captain M. Kimberly of Santa Barbara, California, who fired him with dreams of becoming a sheep baron in wide open New Mexico Territory where good land was to be had for the asking.

Tunstall set off for the Territorial capital at Santa Fe armed with a sheaf of introductory letters addressed, naturally, to the 'right' people. Several weeks later he arrived in Lincoln, county seat of Lincoln County, Territory of New Mexico.

It was a typical New Mexican frontier town with its one store, its dusty streets and its swaggering cowboys and picturesque Mexicans.

Tunstall wrote enthusiastically to his father: 'In the miners' parlance, Lincoln is about the "toughest" little spot in America – which means the most lawless.'

His first friend was Alexander A. McSween, a young lawyer driven by a ruthless ambition, politically active, resourceful and not over-ethical about business. They were birds of a feather.

Tunstall could not acquire range land under the Desert Land Act. McSween could and did. He filed on the Rio Feliz, paid for the Government survey and then signed the land over to Tunstall for $1.0. In January, 1877, Tunstall, now a property owner, went to the town of Mesilla and paid $600 for a Government survey of 2,300 acres of land he planned to claim and he moved into a log cabin on the land to establish squatter's rights to it.

He soon gave up his ideas of becoming a sheep baron, seeing in the Territory and his new-found friend chances of much bigger things. He bought 400 head of cattle which belonged to a family named Casey but which were being disposed of at knock-down prices at a sheriff's sale. It was a start, but his mind was now running in terms of politics, opportunities and business.

In Lincoln three Irishmen, Lawrence Murphy and his partners James Dolan and James Riley, held sway. They owned the

only major store – 'The Big House' it was called locally – had a
huge ranch holding with thousands of cattle, and a Government
contract to supply beef to the nearby Army posts and the Indian
Reservation. They were connected with the politically powerful
'Santa Fe Ring' whose members virtually ran the Territorial
Legislature. And they had the Lincoln County Sheriff, William
Brady, in their pocket.

Tunstall knew that he would have to challenge this formid-
able set-up that stood in the way of his big-shot ambitions.
McSween shared Tunstall's aims and in March, 1877, the two
young men, backed by cattle baron John Chisum, who considered the ever-expanding Murphy-Riley-Dolan empire a threat
to his own plans, opened a merchandise store and banking concern right across the street from Murphy's 'Big House' and
advertised their intention to break him.

Almost at once Murphy and his partners began to feel the
pinch of the opposition. Small ranchers, tired of Murphy's
monopoly, were glad to move their custom to the McSween and
Tunstall store.

Tunstall went off to St Louis to arrange some business there
and nearly died of smallpox. By the time he returned to Lincoln
County the smell of blood was in the air.

To make matters worse the Casey family had regained illeg-
ally, the 400 head of stock and some horses that Tunstall had
bought.

McSween, never slow to seek publicity – in common with
many businessmen and ranchers of that time and place he believed that newspapers were the correct medium in which to fight
battles – had written to the Mesilla *Independent*.

Lincoln, N.M.
September 18, 1877.

Editors *Independent*.

This forenoon my horses and those of Mr Tunstall were
stolen from a ranche (sic) on the Rio Ruidosa. I valued my
horses at seven hundred dollars; Tunstall's cost over one thousand dollars. Two of mine were fine black American horses;
among Tunstall's were one of the handsomest mules in this
section of the country. Good citizens are in pursuit of the
thieves and I hope they will overtake them and plunder.

For the recovery of these animals we will pay a liberal reward. The thieves were seen driving off the animals. 'The Boys' are known.

Yours,

A. A. McSween.

(Of course they are known, they came to San Augustine in this country openly, with the stolen animals in their possession; they defy arrest, and appear to have the privilege of robbing and murdering with impunity. *Editor.*)

The letter was published on 29th September, 1877, and the horses were re-captured soon afterwards.

Meanwhile the Murphy-Riley-Dolan empire was dangerously near to bankruptcy. The First National Bank in Sante Fe held mortgages on their land, store, stock and cattle and they had also borrowed from the Tunstall-McSween-Chisum bank to the tune of several thousand dollars.

Murphy decided it was time for action. He hoped he had not left it too late. He found the opportunity in the unscrupulousness of Alexander McSween. The lawyer had been made executor for the estate of Emil Fritz, Murphy's former partner who had gone back to Hamburg to die. McSween had collected $7,148 on the Fritz estate but he refused to part with the money, claiming that if he did so he would be unable to regain the $4,000 he assessed as his fees.

On 24th December, 1877, Murphy caused McSween to be 'detained' by the authorities in Las Vegas pending charges of fraud and embezzlement. Cattle king John Chisum who was also in town was similarly 'detained' over alleged misdealings in a Government meat contract.

On 4th January, 1878, McSween was taken to Mesilla and Tunstall hastened to raise bail money for him. He also wrote an ill-advised letter to the *Independent* charging Sheriff William Brady, who was also the county tax collector, with graft and corruption.

He began by quoting the Governor's Message for the New Year of 1878 in which, while referring to taxes, the Territorial Executive had written: 'The present Sheriff of Lincoln County has paid nothing during his present term of office.'

Tunstall's letter dated 18th January, 1878, read: 'The above extract is a sad and unanswerable comment on the efficiency of Sheriff Brady, and cannot be charged upon "croakers". Major Brady, as the records of this County show, collected over *Twenty-five Hundred Dollars*, Territorial funds. Of this sum Mr Alex A. McSween, Esg., (sic) paid him over *Fifteen Hundred Dollars* by cheque on the First National Bank of Santa Fe, August 23, 1877. Said cheque was presented for payment by John H. Riley Esq., of the firm of J. J. Dolan & Co., this last amount was paid by the last named gentleman to Underwood and Nash for cattle. Thus passed over *Fifteen Hundred Dollars* belonging to the Territory of New Mexico. With the exception of thirty-nine dollars, all the taxes of Lincoln County were promptly paid when due.

'Let not Lincoln County suffer for the delinquency of one, two or three men.

'By the exercise of proper vigilance the taxpayer can readily ascertain what has become of what he has paid for the implied protection of the commonwealth. It is not only his privilege but his duty. A delinquent taxpayer is bad; a delinquent tax collector is worse.

J.H.T.'

The letter – its allegations were subsequently proved to be untrue – was printed on 26th January, 1878, and the day before it appeared McSween had come up before Judge Warren Bristol and been bailed in the sum of $8,000 to appear at the April term of court.

Tunstall and McSween started back to Lincoln and were still on the road on 6th February when James Dolan and a gunfighter named Jesse Evans caught up with them. Dolan was carrying a Winchester and wanted to fight but the presence of Deputy Sheriff Barrier prevented gunplay. Dolan and Evans rode off muttering darkly.

Murphy put pressure on Sheriff Brady, himself no friend of either Tunstall or McSween, to attach their property in order to ensure that the McSween bail money was forthcoming. But Brady, who only needed to attach $8,000-worth of property, over-stepped himself either through zealousness or on higher orders.

Tunstall and Brady met on 11th February and the Englishman persuaded the Sheriff not to attach some horses at the Rio Feliz ranch which were personal property not connected with company holdings. But two days later Robert Widenmann, one of Tunstall's men, informed his boss that Deputy Sheriff Jacob (Billy) Matthews had ridden to the ranch to attach the horses but had been talked out of it.

Tunstall's employees included a buck-toothed, effeminate little gunfighter from the New York slums who was just beginning to spring into newspaper headlines and was destined to carve for himself a permanent niche in American folklore. He was known then as Henry McCarty or Kid Antrim but history knows him better as William H. Bonney – Billy the Kid.

On 18th February another posse under Deputy Sheriff Matthews was sent to Tunstall's ranch. Over on the Rio Feliz Tunstall got wind of it and set off for Lincoln with his riders to see Sheriff Brady. Matthews' posse arrived to find the Englishman gone. He stayed at the ranch and sent some men in pursuit.

Tunstall and his men – Billy the Kid, Dick Brewer, Robert Widenmann and John Middleton were in no hurry as they loped towards Lincoln. But Matthews' posse were following at a hard gallop and soon overhauled them.

When the posse came into range of the Tunstall party and their first shots smacked into the dust around them, Billy the Kid and the other riders shouted to Tunstall to make a run for it. They spurred their own horses towards a rock formation which offered some cover.

But John Tunstall did not run. Instead, he turned his horse to face the oncoming riders. Murphy's foreman, William S. Morton, Jesse Evans and Tom Hill were the first to get within easy pistol shot of Tunstall as he sat waiting for them.

Morton shot him out of his saddle. Tom Hill put a bullet into the back of Tunstall's head as he lay on the ground.

Then, as the rest of the posses circled around, Hill picked up Tunstall's carbine and coldly killed the Englishman's thoroughbred horse. The gun was passed to Ramon Montoya who gave it to Sam Perry, who placed it by the dead Tunstall. Perry, Tom Green, Wallace Olinger, 'Dutch Carley' Kruling and Deputy

Arch Clement, Missouri Guerrilla.
(*State Historical Society of Missouri.*)

Billy the Kid.
(*National Archives.*)

WELLS, FARGO & CO'S EXPRESS.
$1,000 REWARD!

CHARLES WELLS BANKS, who up to November 1, 1886, was CASHIER of the Express Department of Wells, Fargo and Company, at San Francisco, Cal., on which date said Banks absconded, a defaulter in a sum exceeding $20,000.

Wells, Fargo and Company will pay $1,000 Reward for the arrest and delivery to me, at any jail, in any of the States or Territories of the United States, of the said Charles W. Banks.

In addition to above reward of $1,000, 25 per cent will be paid of all monies recovered from said Banks and turned over to said Express Company.

Description of Charles W. Banks.

AGE, 47; HEIGHT, about 5 feet, 8 or 9 inches; WEIGHT, about 145 lbs.; HAIR, black, slightly grey, thick and curly; EYES, small, cold grey, glance quick and comprehensive; reads with glasses; NOSE, flat at the nostrils, nostrils large and distended, end of nose decidedly turned up; BEARD, usually worn full, but had it removed before leaving; was WOUNDED in left leg, favors it very slightly; was troubled with varicose veins, wears elastic on legs; TEETH, false; DISPOSITION, quick and nervous; TOBACCO—smokes, does not chew, snuffs moderately; NATIVITY, England, with very slight English accent; was naturalized in New Orleans May 14, 1867; DRESS, always neat, collar always turned down, as appears in photograph; HANDWRITING, a good running hand, fast writer, imitates signatures well and readily; BUSINESS QUALIFICATIONS—a first-class accountant; quick at counting coin and notes; in early life was accountant in an iron establishment and also clerk in a wholesale artificial flower-house; was in New Orleans under General Banks as quartermaster's clerk; was in Washington as chief clerk in Freedmen's Bureau; was in New York custom-house as inspector, about 1866; arrived in San Francisco in 1871; POLITICS, Republican; SOCIAL HABITS—was a member of Union and Bohemian clubs of San Francisco; fees all waiters and menials freely; is inquisitive by nature; controversial sometimes in conversation; not inclined to question prices with tradesmen; buys broad articles; is open-handed, has a streak of kindliness, vain of his appearance, likes notoriety, cultivated the habits of a *bon vivant* club man, was very familiar with brands of liquors and French dishes and wines; MEMBER OF MICROSCOPICAL SOCIETY of San Francisco; has a knowledge of scientific names and expressions, although he left school at 14; well informed on all current topics of the day, and few days before leaving disposed of his voluminous miscellaneous and scientific library; is of a speculative turn and familiar with S. F. stock market; has owned gravel mine and a vineyard, and talks understandingly on such subjects; WIFE now resident in New York, formerly from Cleveland, Ohio; he was at Centennial Exhibition at Philadelphia in 1876; is a Knight Templar, and member of Oakland Commandery No. 11 of California.

Wells, Fargo and Company will pay liberally for information furnished me which leads to his arrest, or discovery of his whereabouts if beyond the reach of extradition.

J. B. HUME,
Special Officer Wells, Fargo & Co's Express,
SAN FRANCISCO, CAL., Room 28, 320 Sansome Street.
November 8, 1886.

'Wanted' poster for Charlie Banks. (*Wells, Fargo Bank History Room.*)

A Cornish Miners' Lodge in Central City, Colorado, about 1890. (*Denver Public Library Western Collection.*)

Sheriff George Hindman dismounted and dragged Tunstall's body to where his horse lay. Florencio Gonzales put a saddle blanket over Tunstall and Sam Perry put Tunstall's hat under the dead horse's head.

All this was watched from their protecting knoll by Tunstall's companions. But none of them tried to help him. They were realists, living close to death on the frontier, and they knew that once he was dead there was nothing they could do. To interfere could mean only their own deaths.

The posse returned to Lincoln and reported to Brady that Tunstall had died 'resisting arrest'.

Tunstall's body was taken into Lincoln the following day and a six-man coroner's jury was empannelled. They found that Tunstall had come to his death by 'deadly weapons then and there held by one or more of the men whose names are written herewith: Jesse Evans, Frank Baker, Tom Hill, George Hindman, J. J. Dolan, William Morton and others not identified by witnesses who testified before the coroner's jury.'

The phrase 'others not identified' caused endless argument in Lincoln and also gave the killers a chance to provide alibis for each other. Many men who were present later claimed to have been among the men who had stayed at Tunstall's ranch instead of chasing the Englishman.

McSween, who got his facts second-hand, said in an affidavit that Tom Corcoran, Pantaleon Gallegos, Andrew L. Roberts, George Davis, Robert W. Beckwith, Tom Green and John Hurley had also been present. Widenmann added several more names in an affidavit. Deputy Sheriff Matthews and a Mexican also executed affidavits and none of the documents contain the same list of names.

Exactly who was in the posse mattered little. Tunstall was dead and the first blood had been let in the Lincoln County War.

Justice of the Peace John P. 'Green' Wilson issued warrants for the arrest of the men named by the jury, and Billy the Kid and a part-Cherokee Indian gunfighter Fred Waite were deputised to arrest Morton and Dolan at the Murphy store.

But the Murphy political machine was still powerful. Sheriff Brady had the Kid and Waite arrested for disturbing the peace.

They were held in jail overnight and released a few hours after Tunstall was buried.

Lincoln folklore says that Billy the Kid swore a blood oath over the grave of his former employer.

'Tunstall was the only man that ever treated me decent,' the buck-toothed killer is supposed to have said. 'I'll kill the men who did this to him.'

True or not, it is a fact that two weeks later Dick Brewer, Tunstall's old foreman, rode out of Lincoln at the head of a ten-man posse which included Billy the Kid. They were heavily armed and Brewer carried a sheaf of warrants for the men who had ridden in the posse which murdered Tunstall.

On 9th March they captured William Morton and Frank Baker who had been named by the coroner's jury. With poetic justice they died, like Tunstall, 'resisting arrest'. Later the man who went out to bury them claimed he found eleven bullet holes in each body which indicated an execution by the eleven-man posse.

On 1st April Sheriff Brady, and deputies Billy Matthews, 'Dad' Peppin and George Hindman were walking towards the courthouse in the morning sun. As they passed a low wall running by the McSween-Tunstall store five rifles – one of them belonging to Billy the Kid – belched fire. Brady was killed outright. Hindman was mortally wounded and died within the hour. Matthews and Peppin escaped.

On 4th April Dick Brewer and twelve men ambushed crippled gunfighter Andrew L. Roberts – also said to have been in on the Tunstall killing. In the uneven fight that followed he was killed. But not before he had shot Brewer dead with a rifle shot from over a hundred yards, put a bullet through John Middleton's chest and shot the trigger finger off George Coe.

The Lincoln County War was a series of ambushes, traps and stand-up fights in which at least twenty men were killed. In July the McSween men were beseiged in the lawyer's house in Lincoln and during the fight McSween himself was killed. The military were called in and to all intents and purposes the War came to an end. Even so, odd outbreaks of violence directly attributable to the war continued for nearly two years.

Claims against the American Government dragged on for far

longer than the War as the elder Tunstall in London wrote letters and filed claims for compensation for the 'irreparable loss' of his son. He sued for $150,000 and was still trying to get some action when he died in 1882. His daughter Emily continued the fight, even publishing a booklet on the affair called *Resume of Facts*. Finally, in 1885, Secretary of State Thomas F. Bayard informed her that the United States Government refuted her claim for damages.

Today John Tunstall's grave in Lincoln is a tourist attraction and every year there is a fiesta in which Tunstall's murder is re-enacted along with the killing of Sheriff Brady and many other aspects of the 'Lincoln County War'.

John Tunstall – the ambitious Londoner – like Billy the Kid – the homicidal New York slum urchin – has passed into New Mexican history and folklore.

CHAPTER NINETEEN

THE RANCHER

RICHARD B. TOWNSHEND was freshly graduated from Trinity
College, Cambridge, when he arrived in Colorado to start a
ranch. The young Englishman was completely green – but, unlike many of his kind, he was prepared to learn from the ranch
hands he hired. He had been born in 1846 and had won a
scholarship to Cambridge at the age of nineteen. He was barely
twenty-three when he arrived in the West.

Townshend made a success of his ranch from the beginning
and after being established for nearly ten years decided to stock
it with blooded horses. He planned to buy the horses in Texas
and trail them to his Colorado ranch via New Mexico. Some he
would sell in the new mining town of Leadville at the end of the
journey. The best he would keep for his own use.

He journeyed to Texas and made his selection from some of
the finest horses in the state. Then he hired a crew of Mexican
cowboys to help him drive the herd back to Colorado. They
crossed the Texas-New Mexico border in late June, 1879, and
Townshend was given a note to rancher Hugh M. Beckwith in
the Seven Rivers region by a mutual friend. Beckwith, a tough
old frontiersman who had shot down a son-in-law of whom he
disapproved, was a good man to know in that part of wild and
rugged New Mexico.

The young English rancher was glad that he would at least
have one contact in the territory because the Lincoln County
War, while officially over, was still fresh in men's minds. One of
Beckwith's sons, Robert W., had been in on the killing of the
Englishman John Tunstall and had been killed himself later in
the War. Roving bands of cattle thieves and outlaws still clashed
with posses of lawmen and with each other.

Townshend met up with Beckwith and stayed at his ranch for

162

several days. The elderly rancher liked to talk about England and listened for hours to stories of London and hunting in the country with hounds. He told Townshend that he had bought a piano for $400 for his two daughters and boasted that it was the first piano to be brought west of the Pecos River.

'He was quite pathetic in his earnestness over the redeeming virtues of the domestic piano,' Townshend said later. 'One could hardly tell him that elementary civilization demanded that one should refrain from shooting one's daughter's husband even more peremptorily than one should give her a piano.'

Beckwith warned Townshend that he would probably run into Billy the Kid and his rustler band or into one of the other bands of horse thieves as he travelled westwards across New Mexico. He told him a great deal about the Kid and his reputation; about the killing of Tunstall; and of the Lincoln County War in general.

As he was leaving, Beckwith handed Townshend a note to give the Kid, should they happen to meet. It was a sort of passport through the Kid's 'territory'.

Early in July the trail herd went into camp near Fort Stanton, New Mexico. One noon a vaquero raced into camp to tell Townshend that a band of outlaws was about to take possession of the horses. The Englishman saddled up and rode out to where the herd was being held. Four riders were coming towards him at a brisk trot. He was hoping to placate them so invited them over to the camp for dinner.

'Besides their revolvers they carried Winchesters of the very newest and latest model, and they wore two belts apiece stuffed with cartridges,' Townshend recalled later.

He did not realise that the youngest of the four was Billy the Kid, but was quite taken with his youth and his courteous manner.

'He was quite boyish looking, not more than twenty, perhaps, slight made and lithe and very quick in his movements, with a curiously aloof and restless eye like that of an untamed wild animal in cage,' Townshend said. 'His eyes were never still an instant, but roved perpetually over his surroundings and occasionally met mine for a fraction of a second, only to be instantly shifted. If I were to describe him as "foxy" it would come as near his expression as I can get.'

After the meal Townshend and the four men rode out to the herd. The Englishman found that they had manoeuvred him – almost without him being aware of it – into a position where he was between Billy the Kid and one of the outlaws while the other two brought up the rear. The Kid asked him where he had bought the horses and how much he had paid for them. Townshend answered warily, wondering what was coming next.

'What'll you take for the lot?' the Kid asked.

'They're not for sale,' Townshend told him. 'As I just now explained to you, they're going to Leadville. It would not pay me to dispose of them here. They cost me $15 a head in Texas, they might fetch $25, perhaps, here, but I hope to realise $50 to $60 in the mines. Therefore, it is no object to me to sell any of them along the road.'

He purposely gave the buying price as a lower one than he had in fact paid, 'so as not to excite cupidity' as he put it later. At the same moment he suddenly realised that the young outlaw was in fact Billy the Kid who he had heard so much about. He dug into his jacket and pulled out the letter Beckwith had given to him.

'Billy the Kid took the letter in his two hands and with obvious difficulty tried to decipher its scrawl,' Townshend recalled. They rode on, the other three men watching the Kid curiously.

'Seems as how Mr Beckwith is quite a friend of yours,' Billy said at length. 'Friend of mine too, so it's just as well . . .' he paused, 'just as well for all parties that there hasn't been any misunderstanding.'

Soon afterwards he wheeled his horse away from Townshend and reined in. The three men with him followed suit.

'I wish you luck,' the Kid told Townshend. 'I hope you'll get 'em safe to Leadville and a good price for 'em when you get there, and if you see anybody along the road as wants to interfere with you, just refer 'em to Billy the Kid.'

Townshend breathed a sigh of relief as the four riders disappeared into the distance. He had had a narrow escape from losing his entire herd – and with it his fortune, such as it was. Ever afterwards he was prone to speak well of Billy the Kid. 'To me,' he said, 'he had been a mitigated ruffian.'

Townshend sold his horses for a profit and after some years

ranching in the West he returned to England and turned to teaching.

He became an Assistant Master at Bath College and by 1891 was living in Oxford. At the outbreak of the First World War he became an instructor in rifle shooting at Oxford University, but his health cracked in 1916 and he had to give it up. The last few years of his life were spent in assembling notes for two books on his life. The first one had been published and he had started work on the second when he died in Oxford, on 28th April, 1923, at the age of 77. His wife Dorothea finished the book from his papers. The two autobiographical tales gained recognition as being among the best and most literate of the books written by old timers who had known the West when it was wild.

CHAPTER TWENTY

THE COWBOY

ON A cold and windy September day in 1872 a lean and pale-faced youth named Frank Collinson leaned over the rail of the Black Star Line steamship *San Marcos* and waved to his family. An hour later the ship slipped out of the Liverpool docks and headed for Galveston, Texas. It was the beginning of Collinson's great adventure.

Fired by stories of Texas in the letters of a relative, young Walter James Collinson had thought of nothing but the wide open spaces for months. He was born on 13th November, 1855, and went to school near his home at Beverly, near Hull, in Yorkshire. Eventually his family could take his Texas talk no longer. He had been lassoing the gate posts for weeks and all his pocket money went on books and pamphlets about the Wild West. His mother had reservations about letting the brash young nineteen-year-old loose in the West but she need not have worried.

For Frank Collinson survived the roughest of frontier days and lived to the ripe old age of 87, a highly-respected and successful Yorkshireman-turned-Texan.

He went to work for Will Noonan near Castroville, Texas, and soon shaped up to be a first-class cowboy. Before his twenty-first birthday he had made a trail drive to the Sioux Indian Agency at Pine Ridge, South Dakota; he had seen the rough and ready Dodge City, then little more than a few stockyards, but destined to be the Queen of the Cowtowns in Kansas; he had talked to Red Cloud, the mighty leader of the fighting Sioux who were then living on a reservation, at peace with the white man.

Soon after returning from the trail drive Frank Collinson decided that cowboying at forty dollars a month and found was not exciting enough for him. The great, shambling buffalo herds were being slaughtered by hunters who sold the hides to traders in Dodge City. Collinson quit his job, bought a heavy calibre buffalo gun and joined the hunters on the Texas plains.

Small bands of buffalo hunters braved the might of the Comanches and Kiowas in pursuit of the herds. It was a tough and rugged life, but it was completely to Collinson's liking. He joined up with a man who called himself Jim White, a name he had assumed after a shooting scrape in New Mexico. He was an experienced frontiersman who had fought the Sioux in Montana and had seen out the worst days at Fort Phil Kearny, Wyoming. He had been one of the defenders at the Wagon Box Fight in August, 1867, and had helped build Fort Union in New Mexico. Collinson learned a great deal of plains lore from him.

The Comanches and Kiowas had failed to destroy the buffalo hunters at the Battle of Adobe Walls a few months before Collinson joined up with Jim White. He talked with Billy Dixon, 'Bat' Masterson and fellow Englishman Harry Armitage who had lived through the siege and learned what to expect from the Indian warriors. Soon he was as good a buffalo hunter as the best native-born American in Texas. Once he killed one hundred and twenty-one of the animals from a single stand and his skinners had work for several days preparing the hides to be hauled to Dodge City.

Frank Collinson hunted on the plains for eighteen months and never had any serious trouble with the Indians.

But by the spring of 1877 the Comanches and Kiowas were active again. Their war parties raided among the hunters' camps with increased ferocity. It was the desperate last stand of a people who would soon be penned on reservations, their fighting power broken for ever. In February they attacked the camp of John Cook and Rankin Moore but were driven off. The same day they killed a popular hunter named Marshal Soule and sent a dozen other hunters fleeing to Rath's trading post. Bill Devins's camp was attacked, but he escaped leaving all his hides, supplies and ammunition behind.

The hunters gathered angrily at Charlie Rath's trading post on Double Mountain Creek. There was bitter talk against the Army who were failing to protect the hunters. Finally, they fell to talking of making a raid against the Comanches and doing what the Army had so far failed to do.

Jim Campbell, the doughty Scots hunter who had fought at
the Battle of Adobe Walls, was chosen as leader because of his
long experience as an Indian fighter. Frank Collinson listened
to the talk and decided to go along too. The hunters filled five
wagons with food, ammunition, oats for their horses and a barrel
of whisky for themselves.

'Our guide was Spotted Jack, a tall, dark-skinned, black-eyed
man, part Indian, part Negro, and part white,' Frank Collinson
recalled many years later. 'He had lived with the Comanches
most of his younger life and was a fine scout, a good shot, and
a great whisky drinker.'

The avengers left Rath's post on 31st March, 1877, determined to teach the Indians a harsh lesson and put an end to their
depredations.

'The spring weather was fine for an outing, and I rode my good
horse over virgin territory, glad I was alive, and looking forward
to the scalp hunt,' Collinson said. 'I thought that before it was
over I might have a scalp or two hanging from my saddle
horn.

'I might send one of them home to my folks back in England
to give them an idea of the wild and woolly West in far-off
Texas.'

Two nights out of Rath's the scouts reported Indian tracks
leading towards Yellow House Draw, a dried-up river bed which
was named after a ruined and abandoned mud house, the former
home of a daring buffalo hunter who had built it as a base from
which to hunt in hostile Indian territory. Spotted Jack, riding
far ahead of the party, found the Comanche village in the bottom
of the draw and rode back to report its size.

The hunters cleaned and primed their guns and checked their
gear. Tomorrow they would be in action. The whisky barrel was
opened and the men drank their fill.

Collinson remembered: 'There was much excitement in camp
that night. It was like a picnic. The men felt that the big fight
would soon be coming and celebrated accordingly. The more
they drank, the more scalps they envisioned as souvenirs. By
early morning, when we headed up the draw, many of them were
still "half-shot".'

Spotted Jack rode to the very mouth of the draw and reined

in his horse. Jim Campbell spurred forward to join him. The
Comanche village was just stirring in the early morning light.

Jim Campbell stepped down from his horse and tightened the
cinch. A hundred yards behind him the rest of the avengers did
the same. Then Campbell jumped back into the saddle, waved his
arm to the others and charged straight into the mouth of Yellow
House Draw.

'As we rode around the bend we could see the Indian tipis
ahead of us,' Collinson recalled. 'Spotted Jack was in the lead.
Some of the men left their horses and ran up the side of the
draw and began to shoot over the heads of the men still on
horseback.

'We were about a hundred yards from the Indian camp, and
the bullets were coming thick and fast. We could see no Indians,
but they were evidently shooting at us from behind the tipis.'

Spotted Jack was the first to fall. Another hunter pitched from
his horse as a Comanche bullet found its mark. The thick smoke
from the black powder of the heavy buffalo guns swirled up the
valley as the hunters raced in and out of the camp.

Then Jim Campbell called for a withdrawal.

The hunters wheeled their horses and rode back up the canyon.
Smokey Thompson, an old-time hunter whose saddle was decor-
ated with Comanche scalps taken in past battles, was the last
man out.

Campbell ordered him to take half the men back into Yellow
House Draw to flush out any Indians while the rest of the men
forted up in case of a Comanche counter-attack.

'We could see no Indians but we rode back anyway, shooting
at the tipis,' Collinson said. 'This time there were no answering
shots. We continued forward and found the Indians gone, the
tipis full of holes, and a few dead horses on the ground.

'Far up the west end of the draw we could see a faint trail of
dust left by the fleeing Indians. We burned the tipis and rode
back to Campbell who still held the hill.'

The Battle of Yellow House Draw was over. But it was only
the first battle of the private, non-military war waged by the
buffalo hunters against the Comanches.

'We didn't have an opportunity to be very heroic,' said Collinson. 'If our men had been sober and properly lead, we could

have whipped half the Comanche tribe. But who could handle thirty or forty half-drunk buffalo hunters?

'We got licked and well licked.'

The hunters set off on another expedition against the Comanches. Again Jim Campbell led them but Frank Collinson did not go along. He went instead to Fort Griffin, a rough and ready fort and town where many of the buffalo hunters fitted out for expeditions into Indian territory.

There he met Captain Lee and agreed to guide him against the Comanches. They agreed to meet at Collinson's camp in ten days' time and Lee duly arrived with two troops of the Tenth Cavalry, a Negro Regiment which, with its sister regiment the Ninth Cavalry, did much to subdue the hostile Comanches in Texas and later the Apaches in Arizona.

Guided by Tonkawa Indian scouts they headed for Yellow House Draw once more. The Indians found Comanche trail as they approached the lake and the troopers prepared for a fight. But when they finally found the Comanche village it was hard to tell who was the more surprised. The troops had not thought that the Indians were so close by and the Comanches were obviously unaware that there were any troops in the vicinity.

'The Comanche Chief jumped on his horse, pulled a woman up behind him, and headed up the draw,' Collinson recalled. 'The top sergeant of Captain Lee's troop jumped into the lead after the fleeing Indians. He made a handsome picture on his fine horse. He had black, curly hair and long black whiskers, with shaved chin. Captain Lee, myself, and ten or twelve cavalrymen were close behind the sergeant, who kept trying to work his carbine. For some reason he was unable to shoot.'

The Indian suddenly turned in his saddle and fired his Winchester backwards over the woman's neck. His bullet hit the sergeant squarely in the forehead and flung him off his horse. The troops opened fire together and the Comanche, his squaw and his pony were literally shot to pieces.

'We went back to where the sergeant lay and found that the cartridge had hung in his carbine,' Collinson said. 'He had been unable to pull the lever or extract the cartridge. He had also carried a good regulation Colt, and we wondered why he had not dropped his rifle and used his pistol.'

It was Frank Collinson's last bout with the Comanches. The buffalo were just about played out and the hunters had to find a new way of earning a living. Jim White, Collinson's partner, decided to return to the Sioux hunting grounds and rode north. He was killed in Montana in 1881 by a small war party.

Collinson was visiting a rancher friend when he ran into Pitser Chisum, brother of old John Chisum, the great cattle king of New Mexico. He told young Pitser that he intended to ride over into New Mexico and hire his gun to 'Old Jinglebob' Chisum. He had heard good money could be made as a paid fighter in the Lincoln County War. But Pitser Chisum told him that 'Old Jinglebob' was not hiring gunfighters and said that the story of a vast and highly paid army was untrue.

Instead he offered Collinson a job piloting a herd of cattle from Fort Sumner, New Mexico, back to Texas. Collinson accepted and they rode across the state line to pick up the herd. They camped at Chisum's ranch at 'Bosque Grande'.

And it was there that the young Yorkshireman met Billy the Kid.

'One evening some men rode up to the river and turned their horses loose. One of them was a slim boyish fellow. I was surprised to see only a boy and walked over with some of our men after supper to visit with him. He was supposed to be about eighteen, but looked older when you saw him closely. He was sunburned and not much to look at. He didn't look like a desperado to me. If I had seen him somewhere else, I would not have looked at him twice. There were scores just like him all up and down the Pecos.

'Everything he had on would not have sold for five dollars – an old black slouch hat; worn-out pants and boots, spurs, shirt and vest; a black cotton handkerchief tied loosely around his neck, ever-ready Colt double-action .41 pistol around him and in easy reach; an old style .44 rim fire, brass-jawed Winchester. I should say he was about five feet, seven inches tall, and weighed perhaps 135 pounds. He had no chin, no shoulders, and his hands and feet were small. He needed a haircut. He had a pair of grey-blue eyes that never stopped looking around.'

The trail herd was being gathered by the cowboys and Collin-

son had several weeks around 'Bosque Grande' just to kick his
heels with only one piece of excitement to break the monotony.

Early in July, 1878, a group of the Seven Rivers ranchers
who were warring with Chisum raided one of his camps and a
rider raced into the headquarters camp to get help.

'All Chisum hands were urged to get to the Spring River
Ranch as fast as possible,' Collinson recalled. 'I ran to the wagon
and took out my Sharps .45 from where it had been rolled in a
blanket, and joined the rest of the Chisum cowboys as they
headed out on the run for Spring River. The Kid and his party
were there when we got there, and the Seven Rivers outfit had
cleared out, leaving a trail of dust. I was disappointed that there
was no gun battle.'

Soon afterwards there was a big fight at Lincoln but Collinson
missed that too.

He made the trail drive for Chisum and stayed on in Texas for
a while. Two years later he met Billy the Kid again when business once more took him to Fort Sumner.

'He looked the same that year, still the Kid. He was killed a
year later. I've always thought that Billy the Kid was not treated
fairly, because he was the only man ever brought to trial for any
of the numerous killings in that country from 1878 to 1880. I
do not believe that he killed for money. He took a good toll but I
greatly doubt the twenty-one tally.

'My opinion is, if the Seven Rivers faction had not murdered
J. H. Tunstall, the young Englishman, we never would have
heard of Billy. The Kid said he would get everyone connected
with that killing if they stayed in New Mexico. I heard him say
that Tunstall was the only man who ever treated him as if he
were freeborn and white.'

Collinson cowboyed all over West Texas for several years and
in 1887 travelled to Denver, Colorado, to marry Jessamine
Brammer, a Scots girl. They returned to England for the honey-
moon and then bought a ranch in Texas.

In 1894 Frank Collinson happened to be in El Paso, Texas
and met up with John Selman, an old acquaintance of buffalo
hunting days. He was counted as one of the most dangerous gunfighters in Texas. The two men had met in Fort Griffin and
their ways had parted for nearly twenty years. Selman had turned

to rustling which soon led him to a clash with vigilantes. He had got out one jump ahead of them but his partner was lynched. He had knocked around a lot since then and by 1894 was a lawman in El Paso.

'I saw him shoot a gun or pistol several times,' Collinson recalled. 'He never closed an eye, just looked straight down the barrel, both eyes open. His eyes were unusual. They were such a light blue that it was hard to see where the blue began and the white stopped.'

He also saw Selman kill a man.

Court day was 4th April, 1894, and before mid-morning two men were dead. One was a former Texas Ranger named Bass Outlaw. The other was a serving Ranger. John Selman had two bullets in his leg.

Bass Outlaw had enlisted in E Company of the Texas Rangers in 1885 and transferred to D Company two years later. He had been a good and efficient officer and had risen to Corporal by 1890. He made sergeant soon afterwards. Then he got drunk in the little town of Alpine, Texas, and was involved in a fight over a card game. Ranger Captain Frank Jones dismissed him from the force. He drifted up to El Paso and became a deputy under Deputy United States Marshal Dick Ware, also an ex-Ranger and the man who put a bullet through Texas's most famous bandit, Sam Bass, in the big fight at Round Rock in 1878. When Captain Frank Jones was killed his top sergeant, John R. Hughes, was promoted and he occasionally employed Bass Outlaw as a Special Ranger.

Soon after court opened Frank Collinson met Bass Outlaw on the street and the little gunman told him that he intended to kill Dick Ware. The lawman had, Outlaw claimed, sent another deputy into his territory and the officer had been able to collect the process fees for serving warrants.

Collinson tried to talk Outlaw out of the killing and suggested that they took a drink. In Ernest Bridge's saloon they met John Selman and the two men decided to take Bass Outlaw back to his room. The gunman agreed but insisted on introducing them to his current girl friend, a red light girl who worked in Tillie Howard's brothel. Selman and Collinson decided to humour Outlaw and went along. The girl was busy with a client which in-

furiated Bass Outlaw. He staggered downstairs into the basement
cursing loudly. Seconds later a shot was heard. Collinson guessed
that he had dropped his gun in the dark.

At the sound of the shot Tillie Howard began to blow her
police whistle and Ranger Private Joe McKidrict and Constable
Chavez arrived on the run. They jumped over the fence into the
yard and ran into Bass Outlaw as he was coming up the stairs
from the basement.

He shot McKidrict in the body and then put another bullet
into his head before the Ranger hit the ground. Selman jerked his
own gun and ran at Outlaw. The little killer calmly shot Selman
twice in the leg before the officer could fire.

Selman's shot hit Outlaw in the chest and the killer fled. He
collapsed in the street and died in the backroom of Barnum's
saloon a little later.

Frank Collinson helped Selman to a bed while a doctor was
fetched.

'It doesn't take my flesh long to heal after a gunshot,' Selman
told him. And sure enough, the tough officer was back on duty
in a short time.

He achieved lasting notoriety the following year when he killed
Wes Hardin, the worst killer Texas ever produced, a man with
forty dead men to his discredit. It was kill or be killed among the
gunfighters in those days and less than a year after the Hardin
killing Selman was shot down by lawman George Scarborough.

The Old West that Collinson had known was gone forever.
He settled down to raise a family. Later he bought a silver mine
in Mexico and made a great deal of money from it.

On one occasion soon after the turn of the century he met up
with the Mexican bandit Pancho Villa. The brigand chief was
talking to the mayor of the little town of Santa Eulalia, the
nearest town to Collinson's mine.

'The two men appeared to be the best of friends,' Collinson
said. 'Villa often threw back his big head and laughed up-
roariously, and his white teeth gleamed in the sunlight and con-
trasted strikingly with his dark skin. His lips were thick, and he
had a heavy black moustache. His black eyes were far apart, and
his big chest was like a beer keg. He was about thirty years of
age at this time.'

Soon afterwards Collinson heard that Villa had ordered that same mayor to be hanged from the tramway tower at the Santo Momingo Mine. That was the kind of man Pancho Villa was.

Frank Collinson raised his family, grew old gracefully and managed to stay fit. He was still riding the range when he was well over eighty. He died in 1943 at the age of 87. His faithful wife outlived him by ten years and then joined the old cowboy in the little cemetery at Clarendon, Texas.

CHAPTER TWENTY-ONE

THE SWINDLER

CHARLES BANKS was the best accountant in San Francisco. He knew it. And his bosses at Wells, Fargo, the mighty express company and banking concern, knew it. He was simply a wizard at figures. He had worked his way up from a junior clerk to chief cashier of the biggest and most powerful financial empire in America.

It was all quite an achievement for a boy who had left school in his early teens and spent the rest of his life educating himself.

Charles Wells Banks was born in England in 1839 and ran away to sea at the age of fourteen. He worked his way to America as a cabin boy and then jumped ship. He took a job in an iron foundry at first and then went to work as a clerk with an artificial flower firm. He showed an ability with figures and was soon working in their accounts department. He read a great deal and was perfectly happy in his new country.

Then came the Civil War. He did not have to fight. It was not his battle. But in 1862 the Union was in dire straits and the Confederacy was at its most powerful. Charles Banks did not believe in slavery and decided that he must turn principles into action. He enlisted in the 206th New York Volunteers and rode away to the front. They sent him to Texas and he fought at Sabine Pass. A year later a bullet smashed into his leg at the Battle of Pleasant Hill and he was given a medical discharge. He went to New Orleans and found it greatly to his liking. General Banks needed staff and he offered the ex-soldier a job as a clerk in the Quartermaster's Department.

When the war ended Charles Banks returned to the east and took a highly-paid job in Washington as chief clerk with the Freedmen's Bureau which was concerned with Negro ex-slaves and their absorption into the working life of the country. He did not like Washington and soon threw in his job and returned to New York to work as a customs house inspector.

But the war had changed him. It had changed New York too. He did not feel at home any more. He had fallen in love with New Orleans and the following year he went back. On 14th May, 1867, he gave up his British nationality and became an American citizen. Four years later he became restless and moved away from the city. He did not want to go back to the eastern seaboard and people spoke of San Francisco as being a place with plenty of opportunities for a bright young man. Banks considered that the description fitted him and went West.

Early in 1871 he walked in the Montgomery Street offices of Wells, Fargo and asked for a job. He was given a junior post in the accounting department. Soon his flair for figures attracted the attention of his superiors and from then on his promotion was quick.

He began to dabble on the San Francisco Stock Market and was moderately successful. He acquired an interest in a gravel mine and a vineyard and eventually bought out his partners to become the sole owner. He married a young lady from Cleveland, Ohio. Life was orderly and fairly prosperous.

Charles Banks soon became a pillar of San Francisco society. He joined the exclusive Union and Bohemian Clubs and the doors of the best homes in the city were open to him. He was a handsome man with a full set of whiskers, a pleasing manner and a slightly romantic limp from the sniper's bullet at Pleasant Hill. He talked well on a variety of subjects and enjoyed a stimulating argument on any of the topics of the day.

He cultivated a reputation as a *bon vivant*, ordered imported wines in the best restaurants and tipped waiters liberally. He never lost his slight English accent and was always fashionably turned out. His wife saw little of him but seemed content with the beautiful home he bought in Oakland. He had a little sailing boat which he used at weekends for pleasure trips or for fishing.

Then Banks acquired a new interest. He became the owner of the first oil-immersed microscope to be seen on the West Coast and built up a fine scientific library. He enjoyed making his own slides and was one of the founders of the Microscopical Society in San Francisco. He travelled up and down the state giving illustrated lectures and wherever he went he was welcomed and made an honourary member of clubs and organisations interested in science.

His politics were Republican and he became a Knight Templar. He was also a member of the Oakland Commandery No. 11 of California. He travelled to the Centennial Exhibition at Philadelphia in 1876. There was, in fact, little that was respectable and upper class that he was not mixed up in somewhere, in one way or another.

And then, in the late summer of 1886, Charles Banks decided to steal as much money as he could from Wells, Fargo and escape from the country.

He disposed of his scientific library; he gave his wife some money and sent her to New York for a shopping spree; he rented a room in Post Street in one of the areas where he was unlikely to be known and gave his name as Scard. Finally he booked a passage to Australia on the *Star of Papeete*, again giving his name as Scard.

On Monday, 1st November, 1886, he failed to turn up for work. At midday it was decided that he would not be coming in and that the deputy chief accountant should open the safe. He did so. And found that Charles Banks had picked it clean.

Wells, Fargo were horrified. It was immediately decided that the theft must be kept a secret. Certainly it would shatter their reputation. Chief of Detectives Jim Hume was called in and told to find Banks – and the money.

Jim Hume had a fine record as a manhunter. He had been a fighting sheriff, a prison warden and a private detective in his own right before he joined Wells, Fargo. His team of men were all skilled in the latest detection methods of the day and Hume knew that if Banks was still in San Francisco it was only a matter of time before he would be found. He put his top operatives on the job and went out himself to hunt down the man who had shaken an empire.

Two days later Hume presented his chiefs with a report which made their eyes stand out like organ stops.

For Charles Wells Banks – the highly respected chief accountant, the darling of San Francisco society, the pillar of the best clubs in the city – had led a Jekyll and Hyde life which left them breathless.

Hume reported that Banks, who turned to the best brains in the city for his intellectual stimulus, turned to the lowest brothels in the dock area to satisfy his physical desires. There was nothing in the fact that he went to brothels. Many of the top men in San Francisco patronised the swish establishments which catered for gentlemen. It was the choice of the whorehouses that shattered his chiefs. Hume's operatives found that the toughest and most run-down dockside madames knew Charlie Banks, and knew him very well indeed. Hume also reported that Banks had maintained first one mistress, then two and then three. And that when he tired of them he had formed a partnership with four other well-to-do San Francisco gentlemen and had set seven girls up in a harem-type establishment in an apartment in the staid Nevada Bank Building on Pine and Montgomery Streets, a stone's throw from his office.

Hume swore that Charles Banks was not in San Francisco. The bird, and his money, had flown. Wells, Fargo knew that they could not keep the story of their cashier's defection a secret for ever. Even now people were beginning to talk. Banks had been missed from his usual haunts and there was a lot of speculation.

So it was decided to issue a reward poster.

On 8th November, 1886, a week after Bank's defection, Jim Hume issued a reward poster on behalf of the Company.

'Wells, Fargo and Company will pay $1,000 Reward for the arrest and delivery to me, at any jail, in any of the States or Territories of the United States, of Charles W. Banks,' the poster said. 'In addition to above reward of $1,000 25 per cent will be paid of all monies recovered from said Banks and turned over to said Express Company.'

Hume, on instructions from his bosses, carefully skirted round the question of exactly how much Banks had stolen. He admitted that it was 'a sum exceeding $20,000'.

The poster went on to give some biographical details about Banks and gave a physical description of the wanted man: 'AGE, 47; HEIGHT, about 5 feet 8 or 9 inches; WEIGHT, about 145 lbs; HAIR, black, slightly grey, thick and curly; EYES, small, cold grey, glance quick and comprehensive, reads with glasses; NOSE, flat at the nostrils, nostrils large and distended, end of nose decidedly turned up; BEARD, usually worn full, but had it removed before leaving.'

Hume's poster generously admitted that Banks was 'a first-class accountant; quick at counting coin and notes'.

San Francisco society was horrified when the posters went up on the police notice boards. That Charlie Banks should have absconded with so much money! And because Wells, Fargo were only prepared to say that it was 'in excess of $20,000' the rumour went round that the actual figure had been nearer $100,000.

Months passed and there was no news of Banks. Hume was still sure that he had skipped the country and his suspicions were proved when the *Star of Papeete* docked in San Francisco once more. An operative casually showed the wanted poster to the captain who immediately identified 'Mr Scard' – with his beard.

Hume had created a legend among law breakers that 'Wells, Fargo never forgets' and he was not going to let Charles Banks be the one man to tarnish his shining record as a law enforcement officer.

He despatched three agents to Australia to get a line on the defaulter. The Company was prepared to spare no expense to bring their errant cashier to justice. The operatives tracked Banks' progress through the red light district of Sydney and learned that he had gone on to New Zealand. There they found he had taken a ship to Rarotonga, a small island in the Cook Islands group.

A schooner captain told them a great deal about Charles Banks. He told them that he had married the daughter of Queen Matea of Rarotonga and that he was living a most pleasant life surrounded by the friendly islanders. The captain had a standing order to deliver cigars and liquor and *The Times* of London to Banks whenever the ship called at the island. He always paid in American dollars. And he said that Banks was a delightful host who always enjoyed a long talk with a visitor.

In April, 1887, the Wells, Fargo operatives took a ship to Rarotonga, glad that at last they had located Banks and eagerly looking forward to splitting the reward money for his arrest.

But when they arrived on the island they found things far from their expectations.

Charles Banks, dressed in a neat suit of white tropical ducks, entertained the three operatives right royally and introduced them to the beautiful island Princess who was his wife. He had been expecting them of course, he said. He knew that Jim Hume would not give up until he located the man who took Wells, Fargo. And that, he explained with a smile, was precisely why he had chosen a place like Rarotonga, a place which had no extradition treaty with the United States. He added that while the island kingdom enjoyed British protection it was also autonomous and that Queen Matea was unlikely to look favourably on the prospect of losing her son-in-law.

His arguments were absolutely unassailable and when the schooner sailed the Wells, Fargo operatives were on board. Jim Hume, they knew, would be far from pleased with the news they had for him.

But the chief detective just smiled when they told him that Banks was likely to escape justice. He knew that a man of Banks's tastes could not live forever on Rarotonga. And he made sure that the police in New Zealand and Australia were alerted, so that when the defaulting cashier finally tired of his island paradise he would be arrested immediately he stepped ashore in either British possession.

Banks's friends among the schooner captains soon told him that detectives had been making the rounds of the island traders telling them that Banks was a wanted man and that there was a worthwhile reward out for him if he ever could be arrested in British territory.

He knew that Jim Hume had outfoxed him; that his island paradise had become his island prison.

Banks's money began to run out. He realised that he had spent too much of it in Australia and New Zealand. He had to cancel his subscription to *The Times*. Then he cancelled his orders for liquor and eventually for cigars. He did not need much actually to live on. But he was unable to support himself in the manner to which he had become accustomed.

Occasionally news about him reached California and was vigorously taken up by the newspapers.

In April, 1894, a Captain McCoy arrived in San Francisco from the Pitcairn Islands and Rarotonga. The *Chronicle* sent a reporter down to the docks to interview him and he came back with the latest on Charles Banks.

The paper told all and reminded its readers of the former social prominence of the swindler.

'Banks was once the gayest of the gay, a brilliant figure in social gatherings, a connoisseur of wines and the good things of life,' the paper said. 'He was very vain of his appearance and especially fond of the society of pretty women, and was not particular as to their reputation, and the less particular they were the better they suited him.

'From all accounts Banks is having a hard time of it. His reputation is well known through the South Seas and he can get no position of trust. When a merchant or trader wants any work done in the clerking or accounting line Banks gets the job. These jobs, though, are scarce, and the existence the embezzler ekes out is a poor one.

'He is an exile from home, an outcast of society and dead to the world.'

Jim Hume would smile when he read about Banks in the papers. Sure, the cashier was the only blemish on the detective's otherwise unblemished record. But he knew that any time Banks moved on from Rarotonga he would be arrested and returned to face trial. And he knew that Banks knew it too.

In time Charles Banks's eyesight grew dim and he finally went blind. A British representative was sent to Rarotonga soon after the turn of the century and he would sit and talk with the old man for hours at a time. He was always hungry for news of the outside world and now that he could no longer read he depended on his new-found friend to keep him abreast of what was going on.

He may have heard of the death of Jim Hume in 1903. But if he did must have known that Wells, Fargo, with or without the super sleuth, would not forget. Besides, now he was blind, and Rarotonga provided the basic things he could expect from life. He would not have fitted in anywhere else.

Finally, in 1915, the man who took Wells, Fargo, died and was buried in the little Mission Cemetery.

He had made crime pay. Or had he?

CHAPTER TWENTY-TWO

THE PEER

NO ONE remembers much about Lord Delaval James De la Poer Beresford who was ranching down on the United States-Mexico border when Geronimo's Apaches were giving trouble. Those who knew all the facts are long dead. Those who came after only heard them from others and time has distorted much of his story.

He was born in 1862, the youngest son of the 4th Marquess of Waterford, an Irish title. He joined the 3rd Battalion of the Leicestershire Regiment, but resigned his commission to go adventuring in the New World. He saw Haiti and he saw Cuba and by the middle of the 1880's he was a Western rancher.

He was ranching in the State of Sonora, Mexico, in 1885 when Lieutenant Britton Davis staggered into his spread at Los Ojitos that September near dead from exhaustion.

Davis, along with German-born scout Al Sieber and a band of Apache Indian Police, had been trailing Geronimo across the most rugged country in Northern Mexico for nearly three weeks.

'In three days we marched 125 miles, the last day in a hard rainstorm with the mules sinking fetlock deep into the soft ground,' Davis wrote later. 'The scouts, their moccasins useless in the wet, were all barefoot, and several of them footsore. We had been forced to camp the day before at a water hole that contained alkali in the water. This weakened both men and mules. We were without food and several of the scouts were sick [when] we arrived at a hot spring on the edge of a cattle ranch owned by . . . Lord Delaval Beresford.

'The next morning the rain had ceased and eight miles to the east we saw a cluster of buildings, which the scouts said were the houses of the ranch owner and their store with lots of things to eat. Between us and the ranch houses was the bed of an ancient lake, dry most of the year but now filled by the rain. The

Indians said the lake was not more than waist deep; to go round it meant a journey of fifteen or sixteen miles. We took the short cut through the water, at times up to our shoulder pits, but there was food ahead.

'At the ranch we met Lord Beresford and his foreman, who were finally induced to stop laughing long enough to understand that we were as hungry as wolves.'

Lord Beresford ordered food for the fighting men, though Davis and his tough scouts had seen precious little fighting. In twenty-four days they had covered more than five hundred miles, most of it on foot, in the relentless hunt for Geronimo.

While they were waiting for the food Lord Beresford brought out liquor for the Apache trailers.

'We were, I think, on the third round while waiting for dinner to be served,' wrote Davis. 'Sieber, the three packers, and I began to feel uneasy. One and then another confessed to a prickly, burning sensation all over our skins from the shoulders down. Beresford had another good laugh.'

He told them: 'Go down to that hot spring in front of the house and jump into it. That lake you came through has alkali enough in it to take the hide off a rhinoceros.'

The men bathed and then returned to the house to eat.

'I never had the chance to try it on a rhino, but I can swear to the fact that it peeled us very effectively, notwithstanding our belated hot bath,' Davis commented.

So Lord Beresford was at Los Ojitos in 1885. He was still there three years later when the Silver City, New Mexico, *Enterprise* of 9th November, 1888, advised its readers that: 'Buffalo Bill' Cody, Grand Duke Alexis of Russia and Lord Charles Beresford, an elder brother of Lord Delaval Beresford, would be staying at the ranch and using it as their headquarters for a hunting expedition in North Mexico. Unfortunately, the paper was premature. The hunters never came.

Lord Beresford's ranch at Los Ojitos covered a quarter of a million acres and he ranched it badly. He was not highly thought of by the local people.

Alfred O. Boyd, who was Beresford's foreman for a time – though later than 1885 when Davis visited the ranch – had little respect for him.

'Lord Beresford knew nothing of ranching,' he says. 'He was a remittance man; he was a drunkard. He was undoubtedly well-educated, but academic learning is no substitute for experience and horse sense when one is attempting to operate a ranch.'

But if his neighbours had little time for Lord Beresford, they universally liked and respected his wife Lady Flo.

Folks do not remember much about her either – except that she was a coloured woman and just about the best rancher in Northern Mexico. They do not even agree where she came from.

Herman Lindauer who as a small boy went to Los Ojitos with his father remembered Lady Flo.

'I remember sitting there in the ranch house in the twilight with my father and Lord Beresford, when this tall and stately coloured woman entered and Lord Beresford introduced her with all the English royalty flourishes as "Lady Flo Beresford". I don't think at that time I had ever seen a coloured person and I remember not being able to take my eyes off her in wonderment.'

There are all sorts of stories about her origin and how she came to marry Lord Beresford.

Jack Epps who lives today in Columbus, New Mexico, but who punched cattle all over Northern Mexico in the old days, heard that she came from the Deep South and had nursed Lord Beresford through a malaria bout in either New Orleans or Mobile and that after buying Los Ojitos he sent for her and they were married in Juarez, just across the border in Mexico.

Alfred O. Boyd says that Lady Flo told his mother that she had been born in Illinois and had attended school in Ohio. She had completed high school and then run away with a Negro army officer who abandoned her in El Paso, Texas. Boyd says that Flo claimed to have been housekeeper to a wealthy rancher and to have learned about cattle from him. She met Lord Beresford when she was working as a barmaid in El Paso and nursed him through an attack of pneumonia.

Bill Wallace, who still ranches on the Corralitos, knew Lord Beresford very well. He knew Lady Flo too.

'The way I heard it,' he says, 'Lord Beresford was horribly disappointed in love. He left England and went to Cuba where he had a friend named Edmund DeGoncer, another Englishman, who had a couple of plantations there. From Cuba they went to Haiti and after a short time DeGoncer returned to Cuba to sell his plantations and planned to join Lord Beresford later in Haiti and then they were to go to Mexico to investigate ranching possibilities.

'While Beresford was in Haiti he came down with yellow fever and was close to death. Nobody would go near him because of the fear of contagion. Without food and water he would have died in a short time, but this coloured girl, Flora, came to him and nursed him through his dreadful illness and after a few weeks he was well again.

'DeGoncer returned to Haiti and they came to Mexico and bought ranches and as soon as he was set up Lord Beresford sent for his dusky nurse.'

Beresford knew little about ranching. Lady Flo – if Boyd's story is correct – knew quite a lot. If Wallace's version is the true one, then the Haitian girl must have learned fast.

Boyd's family owned the neighbouring ranch and before he became Lord Beresford's foreman Alfred Boyd noticed that the presence of Lady Flo brought rapid changes to Los Ojitos.

'Lord Beresford employed some Americans, rather on the out-law side, and a number of vaqueros, about whose dishonesty there was no doubt,' he says. 'After Lady Flo's arrival things were much better managed at the ranch than they had been pre-viously. The cowhands got out in the morning and attended to things as they had never done before. For the first time since Beresford bought the place, they really worked.'

Lord Beresford drank a great deal and spent more time away from the ranch than was necessary. Lady Flo ran things for him full time.

Bill Wallace says: 'He drank very heavily indeed and some-times he would go into Casa Grandes and get in fights, but he always went back when he sobered up and apologised to every-body.'

The cowhands respected Lady Flo.

'She knew what should be done and how to get it done,' says Alfred Boyd.

They began to brand every second cow with her own brand,

one she had had registered, reckoning that if anything happened to Lord Beresford she, at least, would not be financially stranded.

But all the time she was building up the ranch from a rundown liability to a going concern.

'I want to run this place so that it is self-supporting,' she told Alfred Boyd's father. 'Then the money that comes from England can be used to buy more land.'

In time Lady Flo's business acumen and ranch know-how raised the money to buy more land and also to fence Los Ojitos, a task which took three years.

But during this time Lord Beresford was going slowly out of his mind. Finally he and Lady Flo gave up the ranch and moved to El Paso, Texas.

Dr E. W. Rheinheimer, M.D., of El Paso, remembers them: 'They lived on the corner of Third and Ochoa streets,' he recalls. 'That was sometime between 1895 and 1900. I was a youngster then and distinctly remember them. I remember that he was somewhat of a recluse and was very rarely seen.'

Eventually the family in England stepped in.

Lord Charles Beresford, the eldest of the four brothers, travelled to Los Ojitos to dispose of the property and cattle. There, for the first time, he learned of the existence of Lady Flo.

He asked Alfred Boyd's father what he should do about her financially.

'When she took over Los Ojitos your brother was close to bankruptcy,' the elder Boyd told him. 'He was drinking so much that he was incapable of handling the ranch. Flo put it on a business basis. She paid the debts, helped him accumulate land and guided his investments. In consequence, the property not including cattle is worth $250,000. Half or more of the cattle are in her brand. Those nobody can touch. The rest are worth, at market price, easily $50,000. If you can get her to settle for $100,000 you are fortunate.'

Lord Charles swallowed hard and paid Lady Flo what the elder Boyd had suggested.

To avoid the scandal of admitting his madness a story was put out that Lord Delaval Beresford had been killed in a train crash while on his way to Montana to select rangeland. It is still widely believed in New Mexico. So is the tale that E. K. Warren of Michigan bought Los Ojitos from Lady Flo for $100,000.

Lord Beresford was taken back to England by his brother and died.

Lady Flo continued to live in their big house in El Paso for several years.

'There used to be a huge concrete block for mounting her carriage in front of her house,' says Bill Wallace. 'On top of it were the words "Lady Flo".'

Lorenzo McNellan, who still lives in Columbus, New Mexico, says that Lady Flo built a large boarding house on the 16th of September Street in Juarez, Mexico, in her later years and died there shortly before the First World War.

Not all the stories of Lady Flo agree in every detail. But all the men who knew her, and saw how she managed Los Ojitos in its prime, agree that she was the best rancher in Northern Mexico.

SOURCES

Chapter One

The stories of Thomas Berdue, 'The Sydney Ducks', San Francisco's Vigilantes and Dr Tom Bell can be found in the Collections of the California State Historical Society. The story of William Smith, lawman of Wichita, Kansas, is drawn from various issues of Wichita's newspapers, prominent among them Wichita *Eagle*, 19th February, 1874; Wichita *Weekly Beacon*, 5th April, 1876; and *Galena Evening Times*, 27th April, 1908. The reminiscence of James W. Grahame was found for me by Waldo Koop, of Wichita, Kansas, in an old newspaper clippings book; it appeared in a paper we can identify only as the Missouri *Republican* about 1888. Jack Masterson's story comes from *The Quirt and the Spur* by Edgar Rye (Texas, 1908). Harry Wallace, the musical cattle war participant, is mentioned in several of the books dealing with the Johnson County War and in the archives of the Wyoming State Historical Society. Henry Burbank's wild and naked ride was reported in the *Democratic Leader* of Cheyenne, Wyoming, of 18th July, 1884. Earle R. Forrest, noted Western historian, of Washington, Pennsylvania, told me the story of Jimmy Mercer and the Apache Kid and parts of it appeared in his excellent book *Lone War Trail of The Apache Kid*, co-authored with Edwin B. Hill (Trail's End Publishing Co., Pasadena, California, 1947). The tale of Lord Trayner was told to me by Mrs Eve Ball, of Hollywood, New Mexico, who got it direct from the Jones Boys who figured in it. Sadie Orchard's adventures are part of the folklore of New Mexico and details are to be found in the archives of the New Mexico Historical Society. Julia Bulette and her amazing life are the subjects of the reminiscences of a number of old-timers and are preserved by the Nevada State Historical Society.

189

Chapter Two

In compiling this chapter I have utilised the books of the authors quoted. The study of the English – or, in fact the British – writer in the West is an absorbing one. A full scale treatment of their works is *Westward The Briton* by Dr Robert G. Athearn, Professor of History at the University of Colorado. His excellent book – published by Charles Scribner's Sons, New York, 1953; and University of Nebraska Press, 1962 – won him an award from the Pacific Coast Branch of the American Historical Association as the best book on American history in 1953. I am indebited to it for many leads.

Chapter Three

The most complete, and therefore the best, account of the Adobe Walls fight is 'The Battle of Adobe Walls (1874)' by G. Derek West (*Panhandle-Plains Historical Review*, Volume XXXVI, 1963), pp. 1–36. I am indebted to Dr West, of Tunbridge Wells, for supplying me with details of the Englishmen involved in the battle. A good, balanced and fairly detailed account of the Custer Fight appears in *Great Western Indian Fights* by The Potomac Corral of The Westerners (Doubleday, New York, 1960). There are of course many, many other accounts of the fight – showing various degrees of accuracy and partisanship – but this is one of the best short accounts. Barry C. Johnson, of London, generously supplied me with the names of English participants.

Chapter Four

The story of the English nobleman 'roughing it' in Southern Arizona is told in *On The Border With Crook*, by John G. Bourke (Scribners, New York, 1891); a variation of the English duke, the cowboy and the two coins is told in *The Chisholm Trail* by Samuel P. Ridings (Co-Operative Publishing Company, Guthrie, Oklahoma, 1936); the story 'A Few Mounts' appeared in the Colorado newspaper *El Anunciador de Trinidad* of 2nd December, 1886; Emilnie Gardenshire's rodeo win was recalled in the Denver *Field and Farm* of 8th July, 1899; Howard (Jack) Thorpe told the story of the Englishman who wanted to walk to the foothills in *Pardner of the Wind* (Caxton, Caldwell, Idaho, 1945); he also told of the Englishman and the milk maids and of the thirsty Englishman and the tin cup; the Englishman and the herd of cattle story is told in a quaint little booklet called *Cowboy Life on a Sidetrack*, by Frank Benton (Western Stories Syndicate, Denver, 1903); the story of Vincent and the squatter comes from *Between Sun and Sod*, by Willie Newbury Lewis (Clarendon Press, Clarendon, Texas, 1938); 'My Lord And The Broncho' was published in the *Denver Evening Post* of 19th July, 1899. I am indebted to Chris Penn of London, for several leads in locating material for this chapter.

Chapter Five

For this chapter I have drawn mainly on two articles from the journal of the State Historical Society of Colorado: 'Cousin Jack Stories From Central City' by Caroline Bancroft, *The Colorado Magazine*, Volume XXI, Number 2, March, 1944; 'Cousin Jack Stories' by J. T. Thompson, *The Colorado Magazine*, Volume XXXV, Number 3, July, 1958. In addition I have drawn on 'Humour of the Cousin Jacks' by John Hoffman, *True West*, Volume 10, Number 4, March–April, 1963. Mr Hoffman was himself a miner and worked with some of the last of the first generation Cousin Jacks.

Chapter Six

I have depended principally on the account of Captain Charles Seton, ex-resident of Runnymede, for this chapter. His reminiscence was published in the *Kansas Historical Quarterly*, Volume 12 (1911–1912), pp. 467–9. I am indebted to Miss Alberta Pantle, Librarian, Kansas State Historical Society, Topeka, Kansas, for making this available to me. Nyle H. Miller, Secretary of the Society, most generously allowed me to draw on a list of Runnymede residents compiled by him. I also received assistance from Bernard R. Carman, of Schenectady, New York.

Chapter Seven

The best piece of work ever done on Sir George Gore is 'A Celtic Nimrod in the Old West', by Professor Clark C. Spence (*Montana: The Magazine of Western History*, Volume 9, Number 2, April, 1959, Helena, Montana). Randolph B. Marcy wrote about him in *Thirty Years of Army Life on the Border* (New York, 1874). Lt. James H. Bradley wrote an article called 'Sir George Gore's Expedition' and F. George Heldt, taking Henry Bostwick as his source of information, wrote an article by the same name. Both articles appeared in the *Contributions of the Historical Society of Montana*, Volume IX, 1923, and Volume I, 1876, respectively. 'Buffalo Bill' Cody wrote 'Famous Hunting Parties of the Plains' for the *Cosmopolitan* magazine, Volume XVII, June 1894. *Wyoming, Black Hills and Big Horn Region* by Robert E. Strahorn (Cheyenne, Wyoming, 1877), contains the story of Jerry Proteau's gold discovery. *Wildest of the West* by Forbes Parkhill (Sage Books, Denver, 1951) contains a chapter on Gore. His death was reported in *The Times* in London on 6th January, 1879, and in *The Illustrated London News* on 11th January, 1879.

Chapter Eight

Some of the adventures of Blackfoot Smith and William Mc-Gaa are told in *Bent's Fort* by David Lavender (Doubleday, New York, 1953). Details of his participation in the early days of Denver, and his personal statement quoted in this chapter, are to be found in 'A Statement Regarding the Formation of the St Charles and Denver Town Companies' which appeared in *The Colorado Magazine*, Volume XXII, Number 3, May, 1945. His involvement in the Cheyenne war of 1864, and his warning to Governor Evans, is detailed in *Official Record of the War of the Rebellion*, Series I, Volume XXXIV, Pt. IV, pp. 421–3. I have also drawn upon *Reminiscences of General William Larimer*, by Herman S. Davis (Ed.) (Privately printed, Pittsburg, Pennsylvania, 1918).

Chapter Nine

The story of James Thorp was told to me by his son Raymond W. Thorp of Norwalk, California. Mr Thorp is author of three books on the West – *Bowie Knife, Spirit Gun of the Old West*, and *Crow Killer*. He is the son of James Thorp and his second wife and was born in 1896 in the same house, in the same clearing, where the events described occurred. The Centralia Massacre and the fight which followed it are described in *Last of the Great Outlaws*, by Homer Croy (Duell, Sloan and Pearce, New York, 1956); *The Complete and Authentic Life of Jesse James*, by Carl W. Breihan (Frederick Fell, New York, 1954); *Desperate Men*, by James D. Horan (Hammond, Hammond, London, 1951); and *Jesse James Was My Neighbour*, by Homer Croy (Duell, Sloan and Pearce, New York, 1949). Frank James gave an interesting interview on the affair to the Colombia *Herald* in September, 1897.

Chapter Ten

The story of Samuel Gibson and the Wagon Box Fight first appeared in *Fighting Indian Warriors*, by E. A. Brininstool (The Stackpole Company, Harrisburg, 1953). It is told in great detail and runs to some six thousand words. I have drawn upon this account and also the accounts of several other people notably *Absaraka, Land of the Crows*, by Margaret Carrington (Philadelphia, 1868); *My Army Life and the Fort Phil Kearny Massacre*, by Francis C. Carrington (Philadelphia, 1910); and *Great Western Indian Fights*, by Members of the Potomac Corral of The Westerners (Doubleday, New York, 1960).

Chapter Eleven

This chapter is based on Thomas Dimsdale's own book, *The Vigilantes of Montana* (University of Oklahoma Press, Norman, 1953).

Chapter Twelve

Desperate Women, by James D. Horan (Putnam, New York, 1952), contains a chapter on 'Poker Alice'; Fred Mazzulla of Denver, Colorado, lawyer, photographer and authority on the early West, is the owner of a tape recording in which 'Poker Alice' is quoted by a friend regarding her marriage to George Huckert. Dr Noley Mumey, Colorado historian, visited 'Poker Alice' and recorded, among other things, her comment on her gambling life.

Chapter Thirteen

The material utilised in this chapter is indicated in the text. They were files of the San Francisco *Evening Bulletin, San*

Francisco Chronicle, Oakland Daily News, Alta California (San Francisco) and *Territorial Enterprise* (Virginia City, Nevada).

Chapter Fourteen

The story of William Thompson and his scalp is to be found in the Collections of the Nebraska State Historical Society and the Museum of the Union Pacific Railroad. His scalp can be seen in the Omaha Public Library.

Chapter Fifteen

Much of the material for this chapter has been drawn from a rare little book called *The Life of Nellie C. Bailey*, by Mary E. Jackson (Topeka, 1885). Nellie personally hawked copies of the book which was published partly to vindicate her and partly to raise funds with which to pay her lawyers. In the book all of the pro-Nellie testimony is reproduced – but almost none of the prosecution testimony. In addition, use has been made of the files of the Wichita *Eagle*, especially the issues of 18th October and 15th November, 1883. I was lent a copy of Nellie's book by Waldo Koop of Wichita, Kansas, to whom I am greatly indebted, not only for that but for tracking down other leads in the story.

Chapter Sixteen

Ben Thompson told the story of his life to Colonel W. M. Walton who published it after the gunfighter's death under the title of *Ben Thompson: The Famous Texan* (reprinted by The Frontier Book Company, Houston, Texas, 1958); the best biography of him is *Ben Thompson: Man With A Gun*, by Floyd Benjamin Streeter (Frederick Fell, New York, 1957). I have also used *Glamorous Days* by Frank Bushwick (Naylor Company, San Antonio, Texas, 1934), for some background to the killing of Thompson and my own researches have been carried out at Somerset House, London, and in the records of the Kansas State Historical Society, Topeka, Kansas.

Chapter Seventeen

The story of Mary Richards was told by her daughter, Mrs Patience Glennon in the El Paso *Herald-Post*, 10th and 17th December, 1960. I have used this and have fitted it into the documented early life of Billy the Kid as set out in 'The Real Billy the Kid', by Philip J. Rasch and Robert N. Mullin (English Westerners' *Brand Book*, Volume 2, Number 8, August, 1956).

Chapter Eighteen

The main sources used in this chapter have been: 'The Reason Why' by Frederick W. Nolan, English Westerners' *Brand Book*, Volume 1, Number 5, May, 1955 (Liverpool, 1955); 'John Henry Tunstall', by Frederick W. Nolan, English Westerners' *Brand Book*, Volume 4, Number 5, March, 1958 (London, 1958); Emily Tunstall's *Resume of Facts* (London, n.d.); 'Prelude to War: The Murder of John Henry Tunstall', by Philip J. Rasch, *Brand Book* of the Los Angeles Corral of the Westerners (Los Angeles, 1957); Foreign Office Files 5/1963 and 5/1964 in the Public Records Office, London; *Foreign Relations With the United States*, 1885 (Government Printing Office, Washington, 1886); and *A Digest of International Law*, by J. B. Moore (Government Printing Office, Washington, 1906). Frederick W. Nolan has had access to Tunstall's private papers, letters and diaries and has written a biography of him – *The Life and Death of John H. Tunstall* (University of New Mexico Press at Albuquerque, New Mexico, 1965).

Chapter Nineteen

Richard Townshend wrote two books about his experiences. The first was *A Tenderfoot in Colorado* (John Lane, London, 1921); the second, from which most of my material for this chapter was drawn, was *The Tenderfoot in New Mexico* (John Lane, The Bodley Head, London, 1923).

Chapter Twenty

In his later years Frank Collinson wrote many articles for magazines and newspapers. He was a frequent contributor to *Ranch Romances* and it is from these writings that my material and quotes have been drawn. Additionally I have used *Life in the Saddle*, an 'autobiography' of Collinson made by Mary Whatley Clarke who collected and arranged his writings in book form (University of Oklahoma Press, 1963).

Chapter Twenty-One

Mrs Irene Simpson, Director of the Wells, Fargo Bank History Room, kindly made available to me the material on which I have based this chapter. The newspaper account quoted appeared in the San Francisco *Chronicle*, 28th April, 1894.

Chapter Twenty-Two

I am indebted to Mrs Eve Ball of Hollywood, New Mexico, for much of the material in this chapter. An article, 'Lady Flo' by Alfred O. Boyd as told to Eve Ball (*Frontier Times*, Austin, Texas, Volume 37, Number 2, February, 1963), was useful; as was 'What Happened To Lord Beresford, Ebony-black Lady Flo Still A Mystery' by Bill McGaw (*The Southwesterner*, Columbus, New Mexico, Volume 2, Number 12, June, 1963). I also used *The Truth About Geronimo*, by Britton Davis (Yale University Press, New Haven, 1929).

BIBLIOGRAPHY

BOOKS

ARNOLD, Sir Edwin, *Seas and Lands* (New York, 1891).

ARTHEARN, Robert G., *Westward The Briton* (Scribner's Sons, New York, 1953; University of Nebraska Press, Lincoln, 1962).

BENTON, Frank, *Cowboy Life on a Sidetrack* (Western Stories Syndicate, Denver, 1903).

BOURKE, John G., *On The Border With Crook* (Scribner's Sons, New York, 1891).

BREIHAN, Carl W., *The Complete and Authentic Life of Jesse James* (Frederick Fell, New York, 1954).

BRIDGES, Mrs F. D., *Journal of a Lady's Travels Round the World* (London, 1883).

BRININSTOOL, E. A., *Fighting Indian Warriors* (The Stackpole Company, Harrisburg, Pennsylvania, 1953).

BUSHWICK, Frank, *Glamorous Days* (Naylor Company, San Antonio, Texas, 1934).

CARBUTT, Lady Mary Rhodes, *Five Months' Fine Weather in Canada, Western U.S., and Mexico* (London, 1889).

CARRINGTON, Francis C., *My Army Life and the Fort Phil Kearny Massacre* (Philadelphia, 1910).

CARRINGTON, Margaret, *Absarakah, Land of the Crows* (Philadelphia, 1868).

COLLINSON, Frank, *Life In The Saddle*, Mary Whatley Clarke (Ed.) (University of Oklahoma Press, Norman, 1963).

CROY, Homer, *Last of the Great Outlaws* (Duell, Sloan and Pearce, New York, 1956).

————, *Jesse James Was My Neighbour* (Duell, Sloan and Pearce, New York, 1949).

DAVIS, Britton, *The Truth About Geronimo* (Yale University Press, New Haven, 1929).

DILKE, Sir Charles Wentworth, *Greater Britain: A Record of Travel in English-Speaking Countries in 1866 and 1867* (London, 1872).

198   BOWLER HATS AND STETSONS

DIMSDALE, Thomas J., *The Vigilantes of Montana* (University of Oklahoma Press, Norman, 1953).

DIXON, William Hepworth, *New America*, two volumes (Philadelphia, 1867).

EDWARDS, Sir Henry, *Two Months' Tour in Canada and the United States in the Autumn of* 1889 (London, 1889).

FORREST, Earle R., and HILL, Edwin B., *Lone War Trail of The Apache Kid* (Trail's End Publishing Co., Pasadena, California, 1947).

GRIFFIN, Sir Lepel Henry, *The Great Republic* (New York and London, 1884).

GUEST, Lady Theodora, *A Round Trip in North America* (London, 1895).

HORAN, James D., *Desperate Men* (Hammond and Hammond, London, 1951).

————, *Desperate Women* (Putnam, New York, 1952).

JACKSON, Mary E., *The Life of Nellie C. Bailey* (R. E. Martin, Topeka, Kansas, 1885).

DAVIS, Herman S. (Ed.), *Reminiscences of General William Larimer* (Privately printed, Pittsburg, Pennsylvania, 1918).

LEWIS, Willie Newbury, *Between Sun and Sod* (Clarendon Press, Clarendon, Texas, 1938).

LONGWORTH, Maria Teresa, *Teresina in America*, two Volumes (London, 1875).

LOW, Sir Alfred Maurice, *America at Home* (London, 1905).

MARCY, Randolph B., *Thirty Years of Army Life On The Border* (New York, 1874).

MARSHALL, Walter Gore, *Through America, or, Nine Months in the United States* (London, 1881).

PARKHILL, Forbes, *Wildest of the West* (Sage Books, Denver, 1951.)

PENDER, Lady Rose, *A Lady's Experience in the Wild West in* 1883 (London, 1888).

POCOCK, Roger S., *Following the Frontier* (New York, 1903).

POTOMAC CORRAL OF THE WESTERNERS, *Great Western Indian Fights* (Doubleday, New York, 1960).

RAE, William Fraser, *Westward by Rail: The New Route to the East* (London, 1870).

RIDINGS, Samuel P., *The Chisholm Trail* (Co-Operative Publishing Co., Guthrie, Oklahoma, 1936).

RUSSELL, Sir Charles Russell, *Diary of a Visit to the United States of America in the Year* 1883 (New York, 1890).

RUSSELL, Sir William Howard, *Herperothen: Notes from the West*, two volumes (London, 1882).

SOUTH, Colon, *Out West; or, From London to Salt Lake City and Back* (London, 1883).

STRAHORN, Robert E., *Wyoming, Black Hills and Big Horn Region* (Cheyenne, Wyoming, 1877).

STREETER, Floyd B., *Ben Thompson: Man With A Gun* (Frederick Fell, New York, 1957).

THORPE, Howard (Jack), *Pardner of the Wind* (Caxton, Coldwell, Idaho, 1945).

TOWNSHEND, R. B., *A Tenderfoot in Colorado* (John Lane, London, 1921).

————, *The Tenderfoot in New Mexico* (John Lane, The Bodley Head, London, 1923).

WALTON, W. M., *Ben Thompson: The Famous Texan* (reprinted by the Frontier Book Company, Houston, Texas, 1958).

ZINCKE, Rev. Foster, *Last Winter in the United States* (London, 1868).

MAGAZINES

Colorado Magazine (Denver, Colorado), Volume XXI, Number 2, March, 1944; Volume XXII, Number 3, May, 1945; and Volume XXXV, Number 3, July, 1958.

Contributions of the Historical Society of Montana (Helena, Montana), Volume I, 1876; Volume IX, 1923.

Cosmopolitan Magazine, Volume XVII, June, 1894.

English Westerners' Brand Book (London, England), Volume I, Number 5, May, 1955; Volume 2, Number 8, August, 1956; Volume 4, Number 5, March, 1958.

Frontier Times (Austin, Texas), Volume 37, Number 2, February, 1963.

Illustrated London News (London, England), 11th January, 1879.

Kansas Historical Quarterly (Topeka, Kansas), Volume 12, 1911–1912.

Los Angeles Westerners' Brand Book (Los Angeles, California), 1957.

Montana: The Magazine of Western History (Helena, Montana), Volume 9, Number 2, April, 1959.

Panhandle-Plains Historical Review (Canyon, Texas), Volume XXXVI, 1963.

True West (Austin, Texas), Volume 10, Number 4, March–April, 1963.

NEWSPAPERS

Colombia Herald (Missouri), 19th September, 1897.
Democratic Leader (Cheyenne, Wyoming), 18th July, 1884.
Denver Evening Post, 19th July, 1899.
Eagle (Wichita, Kansas), 19th February, 1874.
El Anunciador de Trinidad, 2nd December, 1886.
Field and Farm (Denver), 8th July, 1899.
Galena Evening Times (Kansas), 27th April, 1908.
Herald-Post (El Paso, Texas), 10th and 17th December, 1960.
San Francisco Chronicle, 28th April, 1894.
The Southwesterner (Columbus, New Mexico), Volume 2, Number 2, June, 1963.
The Times (London), 6th January, 1879.
Weekly Beacon (Wichita, Kansas), 5th April, 1876.

INDEX